YELLOW JOURNALISM

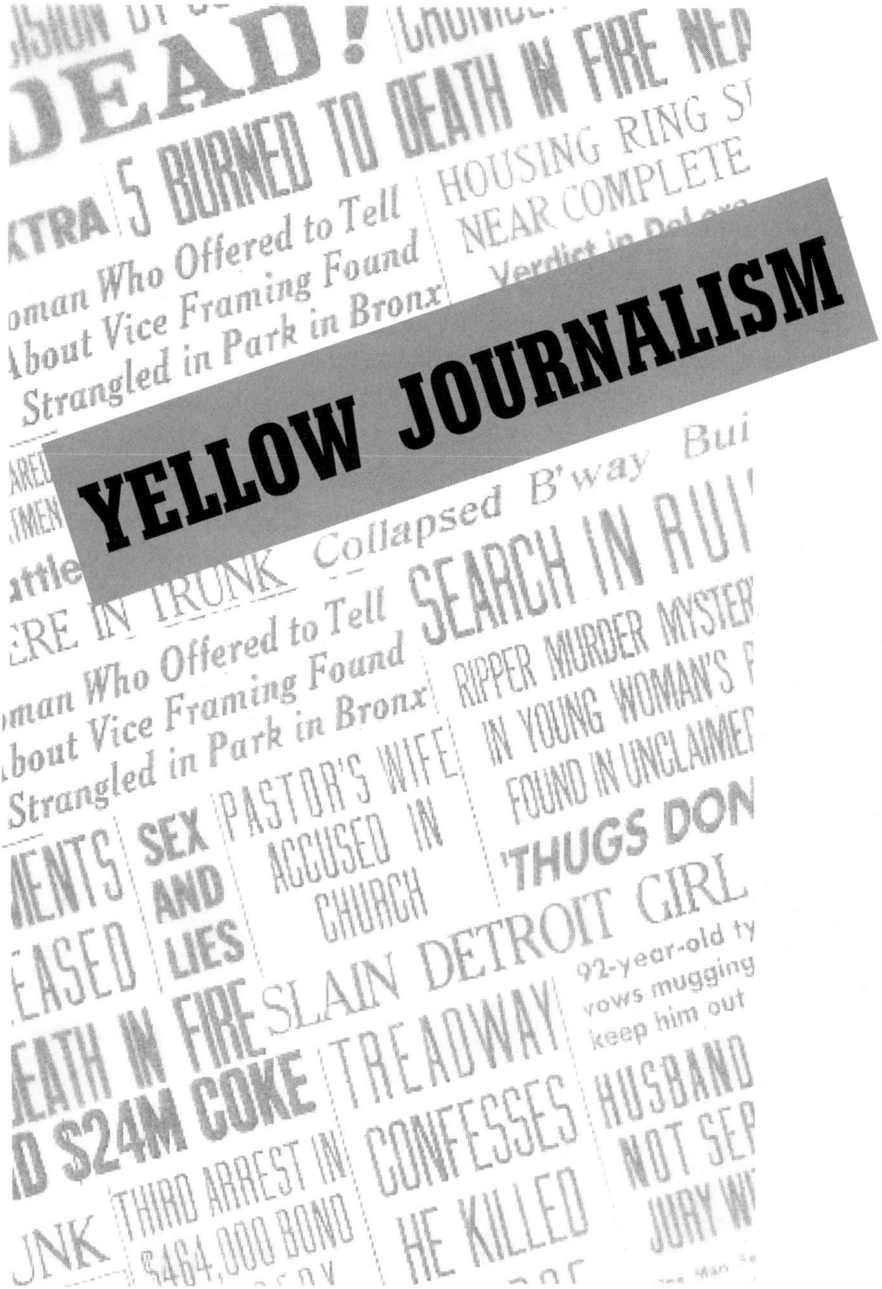

YELLOW JOURNALISM

Scandal, Sensationalism, and Gossip in the Media

Daniel Cohen

TWENTY-FIRST CENTURY BOOKS
BROOKFIELD, CONNECTICUT

CONTENTS

INTRODUCTION
"SHOCKED! SHOCKED!!"

This is a book about HORRIBLE MURDER, **SEX**, THE TRIAL OF THE CENTURY, A TERRIBLE ACCIDENT, A TRAGIC FIRE, POOR LITTLE JIM, THE LITTLE MEN FROM MARS (or THE MOON), and more SEX. And it is all illustrated with SHOCKING PHOTOS or SHOWN LIVE.

This is a book about sensationalism in the American press, or what with TV and the Internet is more expansively called "the media."

Today it seems as if we are nearly drowning in a flood of sleazy sensationalism pouring from newspapers, magazines, television, radio, and even from our computer screens. Commentators and critics point out that we as a nation are swept up in this tawdry tide as never before. That's what they usually say right before delivering the next juicy tidbit of gossip.

Every time I read or hear a comment like that (and as a news junkie I encounter such comments about three times a day, and even more often on Sundays because the newspapers are bigger and there are more TV news/

talk shows) I am reminded of the scene in the 1942 film *Casablanca.* Captain Renault, the cynical and corrupt police chief played by Claude Rains, enters Rick's Café and proclaims "I'm Shocked! Shocked!! to find gambling going on here." Of course Renault knows, and the audience knows he knows, that gambling has always been going on in Rick's Café.

It's the same with sensationalism in the media. We often act as though the American media was always responsible and tasteful and that it has suddenly fallen from these Olympian heights into the muck that is engulfing us all and threatens the survival of the republic. But like Captain Renault we know better, at least we should know better.

The fact is that sensationalism has always been a part of the news, sometimes a very big part. It has been described with many different names: the penny press, yellow journalism, jazz journalism, tabloid journalism, tabloid TV, Internet gossip, and more. The amount of sensationalism in the media rises and falls during different eras in our history, but it has always been with us in one form or another—and what we are experiencing today is by no means the most shocking period.

It is instructive and perhaps comforting to realize that if history is any guide, sensationalism won't be the death of quality journalism.

This isn't a balanced book, it couldn't be. It is not my purpose to present a whole history of the media in America. This is a story about phony stories, snooping reporters, sob sisters, really crazy publishers, ruthless photographers, salacious gossip, and it's also about you and me and all the other folks who read and watch all of that stuff that we are supposed to find so distasteful. Because without us none of it would exist.

In the following pages you will read about the *New York Evening Graphic*, but not about *The New York Times*. You will meet Walter Winchell, not Walter Lippmann or Walter Cronkite. There's Hearst and Geraldo, *The Rip-saw* and the "Drudge Report" and the infamous Mr. Paparazzo. There's Princess Di, and O. J. Simpson, and Monica Lewinsky, and Ruth Snyder—maybe you don't know who Ruth Snyder was, but back in the 1920s she was really **HOT NEWS.**

In a way I guess this is all very educational—but don't let that put you off. One thing yellow journalism teaches you is that you've got to grab the reader. If the reader doesn't pick up the book in the first place, or gets really bored and puts it right down, then the writer has been wasting his time. I didn't want to waste my time—so I packed in a lot of good juicy stuff. And don't miss the pictures. They are **SENSATIONAL.**

LIFE FOUND ON MOON

In 1835 the hottest news story in America was a lengthy report appearing in the *New York Sun* about life on the moon. The reporter was Richard Adams Locke, a descendant of the celebrated English political philosopher John Locke.

Locke wrote a series of stories relating the discovery of life on the moon by Sir John Herschel, a British astronomer. Herschel was supposedly using a new type of telescope so powerful that he was able to see the creatures that lived on the moon.

The *Sun* story quoted the astronomer as saying:

"We counted three parties of these creatures, of twelve, nine, and fifteen in each, walking erect toward a small wood . . . Certainly they were like human beings, for their wings had now disappeared, and their attitude in walking was both erect and dignified. . . . They averaged four feet in height, were covered, except on the face, with short and glossy copper-colored hair, and had wings composed of a thin membrane, without hair, lying snugly upon their backs, from the top of the shoulders to the calves of the legs."[1]

At the time this story was published the *Sun* had the largest circulation of any newspaper in America, and the life-on-the-moon story increased its circulation threefold, giving it the largest circulation in the world.

Other New York newspapers lifted large parts of the life-on-the-moon story for their own readership, claiming that they too had access to the original Herschel reports. A committee of scientists came down from Yale to examine the original reports. *Sun* employees gave them the runaround and they went back to New Haven discouraged. Missionary societies were actively engaged in trying to figure out how to convert the moon people.

Of course, there were no Herschel reports. The whole story from start to finish had been a complete and utterly outrageous hoax, as its creator Locke soon confessed. The "moon hoax" has become one of the most famous incidents in the history of American journalism.

The *Sun* readers did not seem to have been particularly upset by this audacious fraud. It wasn't the first hoax to appear in that newspaper and it wouldn't be the last. In a very real sense Locke's moon hoax was the forerunner of all of those extraterrestrial alien invasion stories that in modern times have become a staple of the sensationalist supermarket tabloids and cable television specials. In the 1990s a sensational and highly suspect "special" of an "alien autopsy" drew a record number of viewers to the Fox network. Times have not changed all that much.

The *Sun* was the first and gaudiest example of "the penny press" in America, and as good a place as any to begin a look at sensationalism in the media.

The *New York Sun* ("It Shines for ALL") was first published on September 3, 1833. It was the creation of a Springfield, Massachusetts, printer named Benjamin H.

Day, and modeled on penny publications in England. There were other newspapers in America—enormous numbers of them, and they had been around since early colonial times. But these were generally publications that were backed by political parties, religious groups, or other special-interest groups. They were interested in presenting opinion, and promoting a particular point of view. Not surprisingly, the papers were regularly filled with scurrilous and often very personal attacks on all who opposed that point of view. Whether such attacks were true or not was almost beside the point. Most of these early papers were sold in advance by subscription, at an average price of about ten dollars a year.

In the 1830s, ten dollars was a great deal of money, far more ready cash than the average working man had available. The penny press was different. As the name implies it could be purchased daily for a penny from vendors on the street. The reader did not have to make any large investment in advance. These were truly the first papers for the masses, the common folk. They had been made possible by an increase in literacy among the general population, who provided a market, as well as by improvements both in printing presses and paper production that made publication cheaper and easier.

What the *Sun* proved so very spectacularly was that such a publication could be enormously popular and profitable if it contained stories that were entertaining and easy to read. Most of the news in the penny press was local or highly sensational, usually both—colorful reports of violent crime were a feature of every issue of the *Sun*. The paper's most popular reporter was George Wisner, an Englishman who had been a crime reporter in Lon-

This clipping from *The Sun* shows the subscription prices—more than the average family wanted to lay out in advance—that made the price of a penny a day so popular.

don. He was so popular that within a year he had become co-owner of the paper.

Truth was not a commodity highly valued in the columns of the *Sun*. A fairly typical "human interest" story told of the unnamed son of a "distinguished baronet in England" who had fallen in love with his father's ward. The couple ran off together, but after the father's death the baronet became heir to the estate. A younger son, however, tried to take control of the estate by charging his elder brother with incest. Part of the text reads:

". . . And while our hero was unsuspiciously reposing on the soft bosom of his bride, a brother's hand, impelled by a brother's hate, was uplifted with fratricidal fierceness for destruction."[2]

This reads like a piece of cheap romantic fiction, which is probably just what it was, yet it took up most of the front page of the paper. It was the sort of story that sold newspapers back in the 1830s.

The success of the *Sun* immediately inspired a host of rivals and imitators. The most successful was the *Herald,* also a New York paper. The *Herald*'s founder, James Gordon Bennett, was different from the founders of most American newspapers of the time, in that he actually had been a newsman.

When Bennett started the *Herald* in 1835 he was forty years old, deeply disillusioned and even more deeply in debt. With five hundred dollars and some credit from a friendly printer he set up shop in the basement of a Wall Street building. Bennett himself was the entire staff. He even sold copies of the paper on the street. Yet Bennett built one of the most successful and influential newspapers in history. His first issue outlined a policy that marked a clear break with the partisan press which had dominated American newspapers. "We shall support no party—be the agent of no faction or coterie, and we care nothing for any election, or any candidate from president down to constable." What Bennett did care about was reporting, particularly reporting of sensational crimes—for this was the news that really sold the *Herald* in its early days.

In the spring of 1836 the *Herald* devoted an unparalleled amount of space to coverage of the sensational and sordid Robinson-Jewett murder case. This case involved the murder of a prostitute in a brothel by a notorious man-about-town. The paper's coverage stirred up so much interest in the trial that when the defendant was called to testify there was nearly a riot in the courtroom. This was duly, and breathlessly, reported in the *Herald.*

"The mayor—the sheriff, all endeavored to restore order—all in vain. A terrible rain storm raged out doors—a mob storm indoors. The Judges and other Officers left the hall. Robinson was carried out of court, and the Public Authorities were trying to clear the hall of the mob, when this extra went to press.

"Why is not the militia called?

"We give the additional testimony up to the latest hour . . . The mystery of the bloody drama increases—increases—increases."[3]

The "extra," or special edition, was pioneered in America by Bennett especially for a really juicy story like the Robinson-Jewett murder case. With the use of new and higher speed presses an "extra" could be on the street in a matter of hours.

Bennett's journalistic vision was broader than mere sensationalism. Gradually he built up the paper's national and international news-gathering abilities. He guided the paper until he died in 1872 and by that time the *Herald*'s reporters and correspondents were among the best in the world, with the fastest means of communications available. Yet in the end, what really sold the paper was sensationalism.

Upon Bennett's death, control of the *Herald* passed to his son James Gordon Bennett Jr., who had pretty much been running things for several years already. The younger Bennett had grown up with great wealth. He spent most of his life in Paris, rarely visiting the paper's offices in New York. For forty-five years he exercised total control over the *Herald* and other publications he owned. No important decision and very few minor ones were made without the younger Bennett's direct approval. He was tyrannical and violently jealous of anyone who appeared to threaten his power and position.

He was also so eccentric that had he been a poorer and less powerful man he probably would have been dismissed as a hopeless and dangerous drunk. He drank constantly and would regularly pick fights with strangers in bars. He would drive his coach madly through the streets of Paris at midnight, throwing off his clothes as he went. It cost a lot of money to hush up the many scandals that surrounded Bennett, but he had a lot of money. He also spent wildly on auto and speedboat racing.

Yet for all his bizarre behavior James Gordon Bennett Jr. was no mere shadow of his successful father. He was also a newspaper man of genius who set the standard for mass circulation newspapers for many years.

Like so many other newspapers the *Herald* always had a dual personality—one respectable and the other less so.

From the time of the American Civil War right through World War I, it provided some of the best and most complete coverage of world events. The fact that Bennett lived in Europe certainly made him more interested in international news than most American newspaper publishers.

On the other side, the most profitable and possibly most closely read part of the paper was a page of thinly disguised classified advertisements from prostitutes. Everyone who read the *Herald* knew exactly what the page was, and it was commonly referred to as "the Whores' Daily Compendium." Yet no one said anything about it in public until a rival publisher, the upstart William Randolph Hearst, made a fuss. Then, and only then, did the *Herald* feel compelled to put an end to this sort of advertising.[4]

Bennett was personally responsible for what is probably the single most famous journalistic stunt in history—in 1869 he commissioned a tough Welsh-born reporter named Henry Morton Stanley to lead a search for the missionary David Livingston, who was supposedly "lost" somewhere in Central Africa.

According to Stanley's account the publisher summoned him to his Paris hotel room in the middle of the night and told him of the plan to find Livingston. Stanley was cautious and said that such an expedition to Africa was going to cost a lot of money.

Bennett replied, "Well, I will tell you what you will do. Draw a thousand pounds now; and when you have gone through that, draw another thousand, and when that is spent, draw another thousand, and when you have finished that draw another thousand, and so on; but FIND LIVINGSTON."[5]

The meeting probably wasn't as dramatic as Stanley portrayed it. As a reporter Stanley always favored drama over accuracy but in fact he did go to Africa and on November 10, 1871, he actually found Livingston. When he met the old missionary Stanley uttered a phrase that is still known today: "Doctor Livingston, I presume?"

There was an uncomfortable moment when the reporter told the missionary that the expedition had been sponsored by the New York *Herald*. Even Livingston, an unworldly man who had been living in Central Africa for years, had heard of the *Herald*, which he called a "despicable newspaper."

When news of what Stanley had accomplished first began filtering out of Africa most people assumed it was just another New York *Herald* fraud. The newspaper had printed fake stories before. Mark Twain quipped that *he* had really discovered Livingston, but would let his old friend Stanley take the credit.

When it was found that Stanley was carrying indisputable proof that he had met Livingston the reporter suddenly became a celebrity. He was besieged by reporters from other newspapers and talked freely about his adventures in Africa. Bennett was not amused. The *Herald* had paid for the expedition and should have exclusive rights to the fruits of the expedition. He shot off a two word telegram to Stanley: "STOP TALKING." Stanley did.

Stanley's "discovery" of Livingston was undoubtedly the most celebrated news story of its time. But was it really news, or just a circulation-building gimmick?

Before the Stanley expedition Livingston was not really well known, even in England, and was virtually

This drawing of Stanley meeting Dr. Livingston is based on Stanley's own material and "is as correct as if the scene had been photographed," he said.

unknown in America except in missionary societies. The world had not been waiting breathlessly to discover his fate. Nor was Livingston really "lost"; he simply did not want to leave Africa. Livingston knew exactly where he was and could easily have traveled to the coast and taken a boat back to England. He did not come back with Stanley, though he could easily have done so. Livingston stayed where he was, in Central Africa, and he died there two years after his meeting with Stanley.

The *Herald* had not merely reported the news, it made the news.

2

"THE YELLOW KID"

"Your true yellow journalist," wrote yellow journalist Willis J. Abbot, "can work himself into quite as fiery fever of enthusiasm over a Christmas fund or a squalid murder, as over war or a presidential campaign. He sees everything through the magnifying glass and can make a first-page sensation out of a story which a more sober paper would dismiss with a paragraph inside."[1]

"Yellow journalism" has become a generic term to describe all forms of sensationalist or sleazy journalism, no matter what the medium. But the term is identified most often, and most appropriately, with Abbot's employer, the newspaper publisher William Randolph Hearst.

If anyone can be described as a "child of privilege" it was certainly Hearst, or "Willie" as he was most frequently called when he was young. His father, George Hearst, once a penniless prospector, became owner of a large portion of the Comstock Lode, the richest silver discovery in America. He became enormously wealthy. In 1886 the barely educated George Hearst got himself appointed to fill the seat of a U.S. senator from California who had

A cartoon commenting on the political aspirations of William Randolph Hearst is set in an imagined White House.

died. The following year he was elected to a full term by a legislature described as "bought and paid for." This was standard for California politics in the 1880s.[2] In Washington, Senator Hearst was considered rough edged, an oddball, but a generally good fellow and loyal (Democratic) party man.

George Hearst and his wife, Phoebe (a former schoolteacher), doted on their only child, Willie. He was indulged as only a multimillionaire's child can be indulged. Getting the willful young man through school was a difficult and ultimately hopeless task. Willie was certainly intelligent enough, but he resented any form of authority and discipline, and he was an inveterate practical joker. His educational career came to an end in his junior year at Harvard, when he sent all of his instructors chamber pots with the name of each ornamentally lettered inside. Even a multimillionaire's son couldn't get away with that at Harvard, and he was expelled. [3]

Willie Hearst had become fascinated with journalism, and after being thrown out of Harvard he told his father he wanted to own a newspaper. As it happened George Hearst already owned one, the San Francisco *Examiner*. George Hearst had used it to further his political career but it was a money-loser and the senator observed, "I have been saving it up to give to an enemy." Instead he gave it to his son.

With the *Examiner* Willie Hearst had found his true calling. As a publisher he had a great advantage–he had the family fortune behind him and he could always outspend potential rivals. But he really loved journalism, and what's more he was very good at it. Almost instinctively, the young man understood that a very large segment of newspaper readers wanted excitement and sensationalism in a form that was easy to understand and impossible to ignore.

An example of the way Hearst worked in the early days was the *Examiner* coverage of a hotel fire. On April 2, 1887, the big Del Monte Hotel, in Monterey, California, was ravaged by fire. Hearst was horrified to discover that his two chief San Francisco rivals, the *Chronicle* and the *Call*, had scooped him. Thinking quickly, and using his enormous resources, he hired a train and sent a crew of *Examiner* writers and artists to the scene. Within twenty-four hours they managed to produce a fourteen-page special edition with three column pictures. Both the size of the paper and the size of the pictures were unprecedented.

The main headline, written by Hearst himself, read:

HUNGRY, FRANTIC FLAMES
"Leaping Higher, Higher, Higher,
With Desperate Desire"
Running Madly Riotous Through Cornice,
Archway and Facade.
Rushing In Upon The Trembling
Guests With Savage Fury[4]

This was not merely exaggeration, it was mostly nonsense. But restraint and respect for the truth were never prominent features of Hearst's style of journalism. Neither was modesty. The very next day the *Examiner* was filled with praise for the *Examiner*'s fire coverage. The lead editorial trumpeted **A GREAT PAPER.**

The famous French actress Sarah Bernhardt visited San Francisco in May 1887 to appear in a play. That was news, but the *Examiner* went well beyond the visit. The actress was literally captured by *Examiner* reporters, who then escorted her and her companions all over town, including a visit to an opium den in Chinatown. This visit was written up in great and lurid detail.

One reporter got himself committed to an insane asylum for a month after jumping off a steamer in San Francisco Bay. He then wrote a hair-raising exposé of conditions in the asylum.

Hearst surrounded himself with a remarkably talented but highly eccentric group of men and women, to whom

Coverage of the San Francisco earthquake of 1906 headlined the *New York Journal*.

he paid generous salaries and treated with great patience. Probably his most notable catch was the columnist Ambrose Bierce, an evil-tempered man who habitually carried a loaded pistol to ward off readers who had been infuriated by his columns. Next to Mark Twain, Bierce was the best satirist America has ever produced. Bierce, who was justifiably known as "bitter Bierce," worked for Hearst for almost two decades though he was constantly blowing up and quitting and had to be lured back. Bierce's writings often got Hearst into trouble, but he never reprimanded the man or tried to get him to tone down his columns. Bierce, who found it nearly impossible to praise anyone, did from time to time have a few kind words to say about his boss.

Hearst wasn't the first publisher to hire women reporters. Joseph Pulitzer's New York *World* had Nellie Bly, who made a round-the-world trip in seventy-two days, beating the record of Jules Verne's fictional character by eight days. (Nellie Bly was the pen name of Elizabeth Cochrane Seaman.) Nellie sent back colorful reports from every stopover. It was a feat that must have made Hearst sick with envy.

Hearst hired a chorus girl named Winifred Sweet, who, under the pen name "Annie Laurie," became the first of Hearst's "sob sisters." There was a "sob" in every line she wrote. Hearst loved her because she was absolutely fearless and would do anything for a story. She collapsed on Market Street in order to be rushed to one of the city's public hospitals and subjected to the absolutely brutal treatment given the poor in the emergency wards of public hospitals. Her exposé was shocking. She worked in a fruit cannery to expose the miserable working conditions. Her stories about "Little Jim," the crippled son of a prostitute born in the City Prison Hospital, were so heart-wrenching that she was able to start the "Little Jim Fund" and raised thousands toward the construction of a hospital for crippled children.

Projects like the "Little Jim Fund" touch on the other side of Hearst's journalistic career. It wasn't all gee whiz and sensation—he genuinely believed that he was the champion of the common man and protector of the weak. This child of privilege often campaigned against privilege and in favor of the poor and powerless. It wasn't a pose, but it was useful, for these were the readers of the *Examiner*.

Nellie Bly's around-the-world journey was chronicled in her employer's paper, the *World*.

Elizabeth Cochrane Seaman (pen name: Nellie Bly) was one of the first female reporters to gain fame.

A Hearst editor described the Hearst method this way:

"We don't want fine writing in a newspaper. Remember that. There's a gripman (streetcar operator) on the Powell Street line—he takes his car out at three o'clock in the morning and while he's waiting for the signals he opens the morning paper . . . Think of him when you're writing a story. Don't write a single line he can't understand and wouldn't read."[5]

The *Examiner's* most tenacious and long-running campaign was conducted against the Southern Pacific Railroad, which held monopoly control over California's railroads. The railroad was accused of charging exorbitant fees and delivering terrible service. The trains were so late, Ambrose Bierce quipped that "the passenger is exposed to the perils of senility."

One of the owners of the railroad was California Senator Leland Stanford, whose name was spelled $tanford in the *Examiner.* Stanford was a colleague and good friend of Senator George Hearst, and the campaign against the Southern Pacific created considerable strain in the Hearst family. However, young Hearst would not back off.

For several years the *Examiner* lost money—lots of it. But Hearst's aggressive and free-spending style gradually built the newspaper's circulation and advertising to the point where it was the largest-circulation newspaper in San Francisco and the most profitable.

That wasn't enough for Hearst; he wanted to expand his power and influence and that meant owning a newspaper in New York. In 1895 he bought the failing New York *Morning Journal,* a rather tawdry little sheet that had once been known as "the chambermaid's delight."

There were at least eight major daily newspapers in New York City when Hearst bought the *Journal.* But his only real competitor would be the *World,* the paper with the largest circulation in America. *World* owner Joseph Pulitzer was a blind, tyrannical millionaire who had a nervous affliction–the mere sound of rustling papers could cause him to burst into tears or fly into a rage. He was also a publishing genius. William Randolph Hearst had worked briefly at the *World* before taking over the *Examiner.* He was so impressed by Pulitzer's circulation-grabbing style that he modeled his own paper after Pulitzer's. Today the name Pulitzer is associated with the prestigious prizes that award excellence in journalism. But the man who originally funded the prizes was one of the top sensationalist journalists of his time. Crime, scandal, and outrageous stunts were what the *World* depended on to sell newspapers. Pulitzer was about to be challenged by an upstart from California who had more money than he did, and even fewer scruples about what he would put in the paper.

Pulitzer was barely aware of Hearst's invasion of New York until he began hiring away some of the *World*'s best writers, editors, and artists by offering them huge salaries. That is what Pulitzer had done to his rivals when he invaded New York a dozen years earlier. Pulitzer now tried to match Hearst dollar for dollar, but Hearst had deeper pockets and was willing to spend his money more freely. He usually won. He also dropped the price of the *Journal* from two cents to a penny, making it cheaper than Pulitzer's paper. Hearst was losing money on every copy he sold, and the more copies he sold the more money he lost, but he didn't care. He wanted circulation. He launched a massive promotion campaign that included posters in the streetcars, brass bands, and free sweaters and coffee for the poor.

Pulitzer knew that he was in a real circulation war, probably the most intense in the history of American newspapers. One of the prizes was an extremely popular *World* cartoon usually called "The Yellow Kid." The cartoon's real name was "Hogan's Alley" and it was supposed to depict life in the New York tenements. The central figure was a toothless, grinning slum urchin who wore what looked like a yellow nightshirt, and it was the first color comic in America.

Naturally Hearst wanted the popular feature and he hired the cartoonist R. F. Outcault to draw the cartoon for the *Journal. World* editors responded by getting another artist, George Luks, to produce another "Yellow Kid" for them. With the two top sensationalist newspapers in New York engaged in a full-fledged circulation war and both having the "Yellow Kid," the term Yellow Journalism was born to describe the sort of journalism both papers regularly practiced. Eventually the term became most closely associated with Hearst and the publisher himself was sometimes called "The Yellow Kid." Far from being outraged, Hearst embraced the title and capitalized on it by sponsoring such events as The Yellow Fellow Transcontinental Bicycle Relay. Throughout his career William Randolph Hearst remained impervious to criticism.

Hearst used his brand of journalism to promote causes as well as build circulation, though often the two aims were indistinguishable. One of his causes was freedom for Cuba. In the 1890s, Cuba was ruled by Spain. Parts of Cuba had been in almost perpetual revolution against Spanish rule for many years. The rebels had a just cause. But the control of the Spanish Empire was weak and the rebellion nowhere near as widespread as the Hearst press made it appear. In the columns of the *Journal* the situation in Cuba was made to sound like a struggle between the powerful and bestial Spanish government and the universally noble and heroic, but cruelly oppressed, Cuban patriots.

Hearst's aim was to inflame the American public and draw the United States into a war with Spain. That was the last thing the Spanish wanted; they knew how weak they were in the Western Hemisphere and realized that there was no way they could stand against even a modest thrust of American military might. There was no war fever in Washington, either. The government saw no compelling reason for going to war with Spain. Each country was doing its best to keep from irritating the other.

Hearst sent a squad of high-priced writers and illustrators to Cuba to graphically record the progress of the revolution. Among them was the great illustrator Frederick Remington. The trouble was that when the Hearst crew got to Havana they found that nothing was happening. There were no battles or atrocities to record in words or pictures. Remington was getting bored. He was said to have cabled Hearst:

"Everything is quiet. There is no trouble here. There will be no war. I wish to return–Remington."

Hearst's reply was:

"Please remain. You furnish the pictures and I'll furnish the war.–W. R. Hearst."[6]

That is the most famous and widely repeated anecdote about Hearst's career, but it probably never happened. At least there is no evidence of such an exchange of telegrams, and the story did not surface until years after the telegram was supposed to have been sent.

The reason the story has remained so famous is because it *could* have happened. Hearst had absolutely no qualms at all about making news as well as reporting it. Nowhere was this more obvious than in the case of Evangelina Cosio y Cisneros, or "the Cuban Joan of Arc," as she became known in the *Journal.*

She was the attractive eighteen-year-old daughter of an imprisoned Cuban revolutionary. She participated in an attempt to help her father escape, but plans went awry and Miss Cisneros was arrested and sent to a prison in Havana to await trial. One of Hearst's correspondents, George Eugene Bryson, found the girl in prison. In Bryson's account she had been imprisoned solely because she had resisted the lustful advances of Colonel José Berriz, commander of the prison in which her father was being held.

Hearst immediately saw the dramatic possibilities of the story. He planned a petition to be sent to the queen regent of Spain. "Enlist the women of America," he said. "Have them sign the petition. Wake up our correspondents all over the country. Have distinguished women sign first. . . . We can make a national issue of this case . . ."

The women of America responded. Among the signers of the petition were the elderly mother of President McKinley (McKinley was still not in favor of war with Spain), the wife of the secretary of state, the widow of President Ulysses Grant, and the widow of Confederate president Jefferson Davis.

Hundreds of thousands of signatures poured in, and the Spanish government was genuinely alarmed, but not alarmed enough to release Miss Cisneros, and after a few weeks interest was beginning to fade. At this critical moment Hearst moved to the next phase of his plan. He instructed one of his correspondents, Karl Decker, to engineer a jailbreak for Miss Cisneros.

When he arrived in Havana, Decker was a man in a hurry. He was afraid the Spanish might release Miss

Some of the famous women who signed the petition sent to the queen of Spain are pictured in this edition of the *Journal*.

Cisneros at any moment, thus making a dramatic escape unnecessary and robbing him of a great story.

As Decker wrote the story, on the night of October 6, he crawled across the roof of a building next to the prison, sawed through the barred window and carried the young woman to safety. Her cell mates had been given drugged candy so they could not raise an alarm. None of these heroics were really necessary, and it probably never happened that way. Decker had simply bribed the prison guards with Hearst's money. They were all looking the other way when the escape took place. She was then smuggled out of Cuba disguised as a sailor.

When "the Cuban Joan of Arc" arrived in New York she was greeted with headlines that read: **EVANGELINA CISNEROS RESCUED BY THE JOURNAL**. Hearst then arranged an elaborate public celebration to greet her.

Even those who recognized the whole affair for what it was, a huge circulation-building publicity stunt, had to say in public that it was a great triumph for democracy. Hearst, who had the master showman's ability to believe his own showmanship, was convinced that he had accomplished something significant in the cause of freedom.

Yet despite all the publicity, there was still no war. That required another, and even more dramatic event.

On February 15, 1898, the U.S. battleship *Maine*, which was anchored in Havana harbor blew up, killing 260 of its 350 officers and men. At the time the exact cause of the explosion was unknown. But in February 1898, William Randolph Hearst knew exactly what the cause was. The *Journal* headlined: **THE WARSHIP MAINE WAS SPLIT IN TWO BY AN ENEMY'S SECRET INFERNAL MACHINE**. It is quite impossible to imagine why the Spanish, who were doing everything possible to avoid a war with America, would engage in such a provocative act. It is possible that the ship was blown up by a small group, perhaps pro-Spanish zealots, perhaps Cuban revolutionaries looking for a provocation. There was even speculation that Hearst's own agents blew up the ship. A U.S. court of inquiry concluded that the explosion had been caused by an underwater mine, but could not say who planted the mine or whether the *Maine* had been the target or not. The most probable explanation, and the one that the president and others in Washington believed at the time, was that the *Maine* had been destroyed because of an accidental explosion in her own munitions magazine caused by coal dust. But such cautious positions had to be voiced quietly in the near-hysterical atmosphere that was being whipped up by Hearst newspapers and others.

"This means war," Hearst said when he first heard of the explosion. And he was right. By mid-April Congress had voted in favor of war with Spain. "It was an unnecessary war. It was the newspaper's war. Above all it was Hearst's war," wrote Hearst biographer W. A. Swanberg. In meetings with his staff, Hearst habitually referred to the Spanish-American War as "our war."[7]

Though Hearst was to live for five more decades, and to acquire and start many more newspapers, magazines, news syndicates, and newsreels, he never quite attained the heights of gaudy influence that he had during the Spanish-American War.

Hearst wanted to use his newspapers to become president. He was elected to Congress from New York twice, and was very nearly elected governor of New York. But he was never even nominated for president by a major party. One reason for his lack of the political success he

,000 REWARD.—WHO DESTROYED THE MAINE?—$50,000 REWARD.

NEW YORK JOURNAL
AND ADVERTISER. FIRST EDITION.

The Journal will give $50,000 for information, furnished to it exclusively, that will convict the persons or persons who sank the Maine.

NO. 5,572. NEW YORK, THURSDAY, FEBRUARY 17, 1898.—16 PAGES. PRICE ONE CENT

DESTRUCTION OF THE WAR SHIP MAINE WAS THE WORK OF AN ENEMY

$50,000!
$50,000 REWARD!
For the Detection of the
Perpetrator of
the Maine Outrage!

The New York Journal to offer a reward of $50,000 CASH for information FURNISHED TO IT EXCLUSIVELY, which shall lead to the detection and conviction of the person or persons who destroyed the Maine.

Assistant Secretary Roosevelt
Convinced the Explosion of
the War Ship Was Not
an Accident.

The Journal Offers $50,000 Reward for the Conviction of the Criminals Who Sent 258 American Sailors to Their Death. Naval Officers Unanimous That the Ship Was Destroyed on Purpose.

$50,000!
$50,000 REWARD!
For the Detection of the
Perpetrator of
the Maine Outrage!

The New York Journal hereby offers a reward of $50,000 CASH for information FURNISHED TO IT EXCLUSIVELY, which shall lead to the detection and conviction of the person or persons who destroyed the Maine.

THE PERPETRATOR OF THIS OUTRAGE HAS ACCOMPLICES.

W. R. HEARST.

NAVAL OFFICERS THINK THE MAINE WAS DESTROYED BY A SPANISH MINE.

The sinking of the *Maine* made great copy for the *Journal*, as for all other papers.

so eagerly desired was his inability to compromise. At his newspapers he was "the Chief" and everyone did what he said. In the normal give and take of politics, where powerful individuals and interests often clash, that won't work.

But another reason was Hearst's yellow journalism itself. It attracted huge numbers of readers, but it was never respectable. People might want to read what Hearst said, but he wasn't the sort of person they wanted to vote for.

One thing Hearst demanded from his papers was excitement. He would read every one of them carefully every day. If the issue did not contain an adequate number of shocks he would grumble, "This is like reading the telephone directory."

One Hearst critic declared, "An ideal morning edition to [Hearst] would have been one in which the Prince of Wales had gone into vaudeville, Queen Victoria had married her cook, the Pope had issued an encyclical favoring free love . . . France had declared war on Germany, the President of the United States had secured a divorce in order to marry the Dowager Empress of China . . . and the Sultan of Turkey had been converted to Christianity—all of these being 'scoops' in the form of 'signed statements.' "[8]

Pulitzer and other yellow journalists gradually eased away from out-and-out sensationalism. Hearst never did. And the formula continued to work. But by the 1930s the once mighty Hearst newspaper chain began to crumble under the financial strains brought on by the Great Depression and changing public tastes. Hearst died on August 14, 1951, at the age of eighty-eight. He was not a forgotten man, but he was no longer an influential one. The Hearst Corporation still exists, though today it is better known for its magazine- and book-publishing operations than for its newspapers.

Ironically the great Yellow Journalist himself is probably now best remembered because of a film. In 1941 the brilliant young director and actor Orson Welles directed and starred in *Citizen Kane*, which was a barely disguised biography of Hearst. Hearst hated the film and used all his influence, which was still considerable, particularly in

This movie still of Orson Welles and Joseph Cotton in *Citizen Kane* would never have been printed in a Hearst paper. The fictional biography of Hearst outraged him so much that he used all his influence to try to keep it from being shown. It remains a popular movie today.

Hollywood, to keep the film from being widely shown. It could not be advertised or mentioned in any of his newspapers. As a result the film was a commercial failure. But it has endured and its reputation has grown. In 1998, *Citizen Kane* was voted the best American film ever made by a representative group of film professionals and critics. The choice, unlike the subject of the film, was not a controversial one.

3
"LOOSE LOVE" GOVERNOR

Of all the nations in the history of the world the United States has the longest and most stable history of freedom of the press. It's guaranteed in the Constitution, in the First Amendment, along with freedom of religion and freedom of speech.

But sometimes, while glancing at the newspaper rack in a supermarket checkout line or listening to the radio or watching TV, you may wonder, "How are they allowed to print, or say, or show such things?" One answer is because of the activities of a miserable little Minnesota scandal sheet in the 1920s.

"In the 1920s throughout America," writes Fred Friendly in *Minnesota Rag*, his story of this colorful and significant legal case, "there were literally hundreds of weekly rags, scandal sheets filled with the lurid and the profane, some of them scions of the Hearst brand of yellow journalism. Some survived for years; others vanished as quickly as they had appeared, surviving only long enough for the editors to fleece some well-heeled sucker and then skip town."[1]

These scandal sheets, usually four- or eight-page cheaply produced papers, were published for a variety of reasons. Some of the publishers had a genuine political, ideological, or personal ax to grind, and used the paper as a weapon to attempt to destroy their enemies, real and imagined. Others were published because then, as now, scandal sells, and some publishers were able to make quite a bit of money on these sheets, which cost very little to put out. And then there were the publications that were used strictly for extortion. Publishers would threaten prominent and wealthy individuals that they were going to publish damaging or embarrassing personal information about the individual unless he paid them off—either by buying overpriced ads in the paper or paying cash under the table. Another ploy was for certain individuals, usually politicians, to pay a scandal sheet to publish unflattering information about a rival or opponent.

One such scandal sheet published in Duluth, Minnesota, was called *The Rip-saw*. In the 1920s, Duluth was still a rough and ready mining town. While the few who had made great wealth from the iron mines lived in elegant mansions overlooking Lake Superior, a large portion of the town was given over to the miners and the bars, brothels, and gambling dens they frequented. It was the era of prohibition and even the bars were illegal, but a corrupt city administration tolerantly looked the other way, so long as it was well paid to do so.

Into Duluth came an itinerant journalist named John R. Morrison. Morrison was a straitlaced, puritanical Christian, and an angry one. He was genuinely outraged by the examples of vice and corruption that he saw all around him. And he started his four-page weekly publication, *The Rip-saw*, to expose these conditions. His aim, he wrote in an editorial in his first issue, was to ". . . rip them open and see whether they are sound or rotten." He called himself the "head sawyer." "A little more steam. Let 'er go boys. Zip, zip, zip, rip, rip, zip, zip, see the sawdust fly!"

Morrison said he was running a "family journal" but some of his stories—like an interview with Blanche White, a Duluth madam—would raise eyebrows even in today's supermarket tabloids. Morrison regularly accused public officials, policemen, business leaders, and other prominent people of drunkenness (remember, alcohol was supposed to be illegal), debauchery, and corruption. Most of his stories were based on rumors that may, or may not, have been true.

Some people believed that Morrison was a good man and much of what he wrote actually was true, although possibly exaggerated because of his own strong feelings about morality. Others accused him of trying to extort money out of them for not printing certain information. After all this time it's impossible to determine where the truth lies. But on October 25, 1924, Morrison finally went too far. On that date *The Rip-saw* viciously attacked three prominent local politicians. The nastiest attack was on Judge Bert Jamison. Morrison reported that some twenty-seven years earlier Judge Jamison had visited a brothel, a visit described in some detail. As a result, said *The Rip-saw*, he contracted a venereal disease and had to have his leg amputated and, "it became imperative to, at least partially, emasculate the victim of sexual indiscretions."[2]

Jamison responded by purchasing advertisements insisting that his medical troubles had been the result of tuberculosis not syphilis, but he never denied visiting the brothel. Morrison was arrested and tried on the charge of criminal libel. He was convicted and sentenced to ninety days in jail. He appealed the conviction, but this time pled guilty and his sentence was reduced to a hundred-dollar fine, a punishment so light he regarded it as a vindication. Judge Jamison, on the other hand, lost his reelection bid in November.

Another politician attacked in that issue was the former mayor of Hibbing, Minnesota, Victor Power. Of Power *The Rip-saw* said, "Victor L. Power's adventure with whiskey and women would not be permitted through the mails narrated." He described Power as crawling into bed "beastly drunk" and vomiting all over his couch. Power also lost in the November election and sued Morrison for criminal libel. Morrison was forced to apologize, but it was too late to save Power's political career.

Morrison accused State Senator Mike Boylan of threatening to kill him. A front-page banner headline in the notorious October 25 issue proclaimed the senator had "threatened to turn from lawmaker to lawbreaker by murdering John L. Morrison." The editor said that in a telephone call Boylan had screamed, "I'll kill you if you ever mention my name in your dirty, damnable sheet."

Boylan responded not by suing for libel–that had not been very effective–but by getting a new law passed. It was called the Public Nuisance Bill of 1925 and was more popularly referred to as the "gag law."

The law provided that "Any person who . . . shall be engaged in the business of regularly or customarily producing, publishing or circulating, having in possession, selling or giving away, (a) an obscene, lewd and lascivious newspaper, magazine or other periodical, or (b) a malicious, scandalous and defamatory newspaper . . . is guilty of nuisance, and all persons guilty of such nuisance may be enjoined . . ."

THE DULUTH RIP-SAW

Editor was convicted of criminal libel for publication of numbered articles, and sentenced to 90 days imprisonment.

VOL. VIII, NO. 17   DULUTH, MINN., SATURDAY, OCTOBER 25, 1924

BOYLAN THREATENS MURDER

BERT JAMISON'S UNFITNESS DUE TO PHYSICAL REASONS

Inside Information Concerning Causes for Voting Probate Judge Jamison Out of Courthouse in Suffering County of Cass

CARHART HAS GOOD PROSPECTS TO WIN

Aspirant for Clerk of Court's Office Is Gaining Ground With Alarming Speed.

ANGRY STATE SENATOR SAYS HE WILL KILL HEAD-SAWYER

Mike Boylan Threatens by Wire from Virginia to Bump Off John L. Morrison if Solon's Name Is Mentioned in Rip-Saw

JOE CARHART

The *Rip-saw* was full of sensational stories, from the health of politicians to death threats aimed at its editor.

What that meant in practice was a single judge, without a jury, had the right to stop a newspaper or magazine from being published forever because he considered it to be "obscene, lewd and lascivious" or "malicious, scandalous and defamatory." Such a publication could be shut down because of what it might print, not because of what it had already printed.

One of the cornerstones of freedom of the press in America is that while you might get into serious legal trouble for something that you publish, you cannot (ex-

43

cept under extraordinary circumstances like publishing vital military information during wartime) be prevented from publishing just because some judge thinks it may be wrong. Yet this bill passed the Minnesota House overwhelmingly and the Senate unanimously. Not a single Minnesota daily newspaper objected to the bill. In fact it was barely noticed.

The law was aimed specifically at Morrison and his *Rip-saw*. In the spring of 1926 he gave the state an opportunity to test the new law. The mayor of Minneapolis, George Emerson Leach, was running for governor. *The Rip-saw* headlined "Minnesotans Do Not Want Loose-Love Governor." That triggered an injunction to shut down *The Rip-saw* permanently under the new public nuisance law.

The test never came because on May 18, 1926, Morrison suddenly died. Without its Head Sawyer, *The Rip-saw* ceased to exist. But the law that had been aimed at it remained on the books. The full force of the law was to fall on a publication even less reputable than *The Rip-saw*.

This publication was *The Saturday Press* of Minneapolis, and it was in trouble even before its first issue hit the streets in September 1927. The publishers of *The Saturday Press* were Howard A. Guilford and Jay M. Near. This pair had previously run a publication called the *Twin City Reporter*. It was an unabashed scandal sheet that featured headlines like, "Smooth Minneapolis Doctor With Woman in St. Paul Hotel" and "White Slavery Trade: Well-Known Local Man is Running Women and Living Off Their Earnings."

For all his excesses, Morrison was a genuine Christian reformer. Guilford and Near were scandalmongering journalists who often stooped to extortion. They were also anti-Semitic, antiblack, anti-Catholic, antiforeigner, and regarded all labor unions as Communist. This pair had absolutely nothing to recommend them.

Some whom Guilford had offended ambushed and shot him four times. He recovered, turned his interest in *The Saturday Press* over to Near, and retired temporarily from the dangerous practice of journalism.

Soon after, Minnesota county attorney Floyd Olson invoked the public nuisance law that had been designed to shut down *The Rip-saw*. Olson accurately described *The Saturday Press* as a "malicious, scandalous, and defamatory" publication. He got a judge to issue an order that essentially shut the publication down permanently. According to the order it could not be published, possessed, sold, or given away.

Near's lawyer advised him to obey the order, but to challenge the constitutionality of the law. Such a challenge would almost certainly have to be carried right up to the U.S. Supreme Court. It takes a lot of money to take a case all the way up to the Supreme Court, and Near's problem was that he was flat broke. His only source of income had been *The Saturday Press*. Without it he had no money coming in, and sometimes had trouble even getting enough to eat.

Then Near was told about a new organization that might be interested in taking his case. It was called the American Civil Liberties Union (ACLU). Roger Baldwin, the ACLU's idealistic founder, regarded Near's publication as disgusting. But he thought that legally banning a publication even before it was printed was far more dangerous than letting it publish.

"Heretofore the only control of the press has been by prosecution for criminal or libelous matter after the offense. We see in this new device for previous restraint of publication a menace to the whole principle of freedom of the press," the ACLU said.

Much to the surprise of Baldwin and other leaders, the ACLU found itself under attack from Minnesota's leading newspapers. The organization was accused of worrying more about the blackmailer and scandalmonger, and the papers said that the legitimate press had nothing to fear from such a law.

The ACLU was used to supporting unpopular causes, but as a small organization it faced the same problem Near did–it didn't have the money to fight the case all the way to the Supreme Court either.

At this point another combatant entered the fray–and a most improbable one. He was Robert Rutherford "Bertie" McCormick, better known as Colonel McCormick, or simply the Colonel. Colonel McCormick was the millionaire editor and publisher of the *Chicago Tribune*, one of the most influential and profitable newspapers in America.

As we have already seen, American newspaper publishing has had more than its share of egotistical eccentrics. The Colonel ranks at or near the top of this list. He was the grandson of Joseph Medill, who had helped build the *Tribune* into a powerful and influential newspaper, and he was part of a large publishing family. His cousin was Joseph Patterson, publisher of the New York *Daily News*, the newspaper with the largest circulation in America.

To describe Colonel McCormick as a hardshell conservative would be wide of the mark–he was a raving reactionary. He was described as having "one of the finest minds of the fourteenth century." His father had been a diplomat (though a remarkably inept and unsuccessful one), and young Bertie spent much of his youth in Europe. He was educated at two of America's most exclusive Eastern schools, the prep school Groton and Yale University. He spoke with what sounded like an affected English accent. Yet the Colonel hated Europe, particularly England, which he regarded as decadent and class ridden. This of course did not stop him from living very much like a European aristocrat, in a manor house full of French antiques and decorated with English hunting prints.

The Colonel went so far as to have the *Tribune* adopt a peculiar "Americanized," or phonetic, spelling so as to distance himself from the hated British. For generations *Tribune* readers struggled with such spellings as iland for island, frate in place of freight, jaz rather than jazz, and photo became foto. So great was his influence that it wasn't until 1975, twenty years after his death, that the *Tribune* gave up the struggle to change spelling. An editorial noted that "thru is through and so is tho."

The Colonel didn't think much more of the East Coast or of Wisconsin, which he called "the nuttiest state in the Union next to California," than he did of decadent Europe, despite the fact that he has been accurately called "the best traveled man in Chicago." He was always on the go—usually to places he said he hated.

McCormick extolled "Chicagoland," a term that described a large portion of the Midwest and not just the city. This to him was the "real" America, a region of solid American enterprise and values. And incidentally, the area where the *Tribune* was the most widely read newspaper. The motto, THE WORLD'S GREATEST NEWSPAPER, appeared on the *Tribune's* masthead.

The Colonel, who got his Army commission in World War I, habitually exaggerated his wartime exploits, but he always regarded himself as one of the greatest military strategists in history—and a genius in many other areas as well. No one could tell him anything.

He would occasionally show up in the *Tribune* pressroom wearing his old World War I uniform, accompanied by one of his German shepherds. His office on the twenty-fourth floor of the Tribune Tower was not merely imposing—it was a monument to his monumental ego. It was 35 feet (10 meters) long with a 15-foot (4.5-meter) ceiling. He greeted visitors from behind a 7-foot (2-meter) slab of marble that he used as a desk.

Despite his oddities (and there has been space to recount only a tiny fraction of them here) the Colonel was genuinely and passionately devoted to the First Amendment and freedom of the press. When he heard about the Near case he became enraged; McCormick was easily enraged, and he never backed down from a fight.

In 1916 he got into a fight with automobile manufacturer Henry Ford and called him an "ignorant idealist and unpatriotic American." Ford sued for libel. The case dragged on for months and cost these two millionaires at least half a million each and tarnished both of their reputations. Finally Ford won, but the jury awarded him a humiliating six cents. McCormick claimed victory and refused to pay.

The Colonel was no yellow journalist of the Hearst variety. In fact he hated Hearst. A circulation war between the *Tribune* and Hearst's *Chicago American* was fought out between news dealers and distributors Chicago-style, with guns on the streets. In a two-year period more than twenty people were killed. McCormick did not hesitate to publish damaging personal information of questionable authenticity about anyone he happened to disagree with, and like Near the Colonel was a bigot and regarded Near's opinions as fairly moderate.

But it was the concept of freedom of the press, not Near's writings, that he was eager to defend. Leading the charge for McCormick was Chicago lawyer Weymouth Kirkland, one of McCormick's few close friends. Years later Kirkland said, "People ask me how in the world I have gotten along with McCormick all these years. It's really very simple. I find out what he wants and I give it to him."

In this case what McCormick wanted was a constitutional test of the Minnesota gag law. With his infinitely greater resources he pushed aside the ACLU and essentially took control of the case. Near wasn't interested in the Constitution. He just wanted to get his scandal sheet back on the streets and make some money. He tried to get money out of McCormick. "I take it this Johnny's trying to shake us down," McCormick wrote to Kirkland. "I think you draw the right conclusion," Kirkland responded. Near got nothing from McCormick.[3]

There were still newspapers that deplored the Colonel's activities on behalf of a scandal sheet.

The Christian Science Monitor, one of the country's most responsible and enlightened newspapers, wrote that responsible journalism had to reject the activities of sensation-seeking newspapers if it were to preserve its good name. The *Monitor* said that the activities of papers like *The Saturday Press* were far more dangerous than the Minnesota gag law itself.

But McCormick used his clout with the American Newspaper Publishers Association to get strong official backing for his actions in the case. Most of the objections came from the publishers of Minnesota newspapers.

So in April 1930 the case of *Near* v. *Minnesota* was finally placed on the docket of the U.S. Supreme Court.

In the end the case was decided by the nine justices of the Supreme Court by the narrowest of margins–five to four–in favor of reversing the lower court decisions that upheld the Minnesota gag law. Despite the narrowness of the margin the decision was an extremely significant one– as the members of the court knew. Chief Justice Charles Evans Hughes chose to write and deliver the majority opinion personally. That gave the decision extra weight.

The Chief Justice made no apologies for the tawdry nature of Near's publication:

"Some degree of abuse is inseparable from the proper use of everything, and in no instance is this more true than in that of the press. It has accordingly been decided by the practice of the states, that it is better to leave a few of the noxious branches to their luxuriant growth, than by pruning them away, to injure the vigor of those yielding the proper fruits."[4]

He said that for 150 years there had been almost no attempts to place prior restraints on the press. If false accusations were published then the press could be sued– but only after the material was published.

"The fact that the liberty of the press may be abused by miscreant purveyors of scandal does not make any less necessary the immunity of the press from previous restraint in dealing with official misconduct. Subsequent punishment for such abuses as may exist is the appropriate remedy consistent with constitutional privilege."

Colonel McCormick was triumphant. "The decision of Chief Justice Hughes will go down in history as one of the greatest triumphs for free thought," he said. Jay M. Near was triumphant as well, though no one seemed particularly interested in what he thought or said, and many of the stories about the Supreme Court decision didn't even mention his name; it was simply "the gag law case."[5]

In October 1932, Near went back to publishing *The Saturday Press,* now calling it "The paper that refused to stay gagged." He hadn't changed much; if anything he

Howard Guilford, editor of *The Saturday Press*, was shot to death in his car in 1934.

had gotten worse. He conducted a vicious campaign against his old opponent Floyd Olson, now governor of Minnesota, calling him a tool of "Jew pigs," "thugs," and "Communists."

Still the paper did not thrive and Near again teamed up with his former partner Howard Guilford. Their relationship was a stormy one and Near said he objected to Guilford's desire to fill the paper with "scandal so vile it stunk." He said that if he had to go "smearing sex filth I'll quit and drive off a bridge."

But it was Guilford who met a violent end. On September 6, 1934, his car was forced off the road by a black sedan driven by gangsters. This time he was not as lucky as he had been in a previous ambush—a shotgun blast nearly blew his head off. No one could or would identify the gunmen and the murder was never solved. Near said that the assassins had been "hired by Communists."

Near himself died of natural causes on April 17, 1936. He was almost completely forgotten. Yet the case that bears his name has had a profound impact and given a whole new meaning to freedom of the press in America.

4

"GOOD EVENING, MR. AND MRS. AMERICA"

Were it not for some recent films the name Walter Winchell would be practically unknown today. Yet from the 1920s through the 1950s, Winchell was one of the most famous journalists in America, and the most influential and feared. It has been estimated that at the height of his fame some 50 million Americans (out of an adult population of about 75 million) either read his daily newspaper column or listened to his weekly radio broadcasts. No one before or since has had such a large continuous audience. No one has even come close.[1]

Winchell also fundamentally changed the nature of journalism in America. He didn't invent gossip. That had always been a part of American journalism; he just used it more effectively than anyone else. He made it, if not respectable, at least more acceptable. In the 1920s, when Winchell began his career, most newspapers were awash in tales of crime and scandal yet they were reluctant even to print information that a woman was pregnant before the baby was actually born and birth notices sent out, for fear of crossing the boundaries of good taste. Winchell changed all of that. He told his readers who was expecting a "blessed event," who was "making whoopee" with whom, which marriages had gone "phffit," who was sick, who was broke, and all sorts of other secrets, large and small, that had once been taboo in the major media.

Winchell concentrated not so much on events as on personalities—the powerful, the rich, the famous, as well as the celebrities, those people who were not necessarily rich or powerful but were simply famous for being famous. And he did it in a slangy, rapid-fire style all his own. Today an old Walter Winchell column sounds unbearably corny, and sometimes almost completely incomprehensible. What is "lohengrinned"? In Winchell slang it is getting married, a reference to the popular wedding march from the opera *Lohengrin.* In his heyday everybody knew just exactly what he was talking about and whom. While some complained that Winchell was debasing not only the culture but the language, most people loved him. One of the tag lines applied to his column was, "Winchell knows all, sees all and tells all."

Winchell didn't create the image of the big-city newsman as a cynical, fast-talking, wisecracking, anything-for-a-story snoop, who always wore a snap-brim fedora and had a cigarette hanging out of his mouth. That image came out of plays like *The Front Page* by Charles MacArthur and Ben Hecht. But Winchell adopted the image as his own and impressed it on generations of Americans, much to the disgust of other newspapermen who were trying to be taken more seriously.

Walter Winchell (originally spelled Winschel) was born in New York City in 1897 to a family of immigrant Russian Jews. His father, Jacob, couldn't hold a steady job and chased women. To escape both poverty and a turbulent home, Winchell quit school and went into vaudeville when he was about fourteen. He was a good-looking boy, a fair dancer with a pleasant singing voice and a snappy line of jokes and patter. But he was one of thousands in vaudeville, and he never really stood out. He toured for years in a variety of acts, yet he was never a top of the bill act, not even on the minor circuits.

In order to supplement his meager income Walter began submitting little items, jokes, and snappy sayings to the weekly vaudeville trade paper *Billboard.* He then began doing a regular column for another but smaller weekly trade paper *Vaudeville News.* Eventually Walter began working full-time for *Vaudeville News,* making less than he had made on the stage, but enjoying it more. He had never really liked being a vaudevillian. He loved being a newspaper columnist. And nobody ever worked harder. He haunted the stage doors, the restaurants, and theatrical offices of Broadway, literally day and night. His typical greeting to an acquaintance would be, "Hi, waddya know that I don't." His column was a familiar mixture of gags, poems, theatrical news, and some generally harmless and self-serving gossip. After a few years he knew, and was known by, practically everybody on Broadway.

His big chance came in 1924, when he was able to talk his way into becoming the Broadway columnist and reporter for an about-to-be launched daily tabloid, the *New York Evening Graphic.* The *Graphic* was the brainchild of publishing millionaire Bernarr Macfadden. While other publishing magnates like Pulitzer and Hearst may have been willful and even eccentric, Macfadden was a genuine crackpot. He believed that all illness could be cured by a combination of physical exercise and proper diet. In Macfadden's view all doctors were "quacks." He thoroughly believed what he preached and it cost the lives of two of his children, who were denied proper medical treatment.

Macfadden's publishing empire was based on magazines, primarily *Physical Culture*, which promoted his principles of health. Macfadden had an ambition beyond changing the health of the nation; he wanted to become president and he really thought he had a chance of being elected. In order to do that he needed a newspaper to promote his political career. It was primarily for this reason that he conceived the idea for the *New York Evening Graphic*. Becoming president was an ambition Macfadden shared with William Randolph Hearst, but Hearst was a lot richer and not nearly as strange.

Macfadden proclaimed that the *Graphic* would publish "Nothing But the Truth." In fact, the paper was a sensationalist tabloid much like the other New York sensationalist tabloids–only more so. The *Graphic's* most notable contribution to journalism was the "composograph"–essentially a fake photograph. The heads of real individuals in the news were put on posed bodies of models, allowing the paper to appear to have a photo of practically every news event, whether a photographer had been there or not. Sometimes *Graphic* editors used any photo at hand. When doing a story on an accused murderer named Carillo, the editors found they had no photo, so they simply inserted a picture of the actor Leo Carrillo.

Some of the headlines in the first issue in September 1924 read: **I KNOW WHO KILLED MY BROTHER** and **MY FRIENDS**

DRAGGED ME INTO THE GUTTER. Then, as now, there was a tremendous interest in Britain's royal family. Heading a story on the Prince of Wales was **PRINCE TELLS ME JUST WHY IT IS HE'S SO SAD.**[2]

The two major focuses of *Graphic* stories were sex, which built circulation, and health faddism, the obsession of its publisher. One of the jokes told about the *Graphic*– there were many–was that the paper was "for fornication and against vaccination."[3]

This was the publication that gave Walter Winchell his first exposure beyond the entertainment community. At first his column was almost identical to the sort of thing he had already been doing: It was filled with jokes, anecdotes, often told in Broadway slang, and sometimes sentimental poems submitted by readers. There was also a little mild gossip, announcing marriages and births after they happened. The items were generally flattering. But within a few weeks Winchell began using material that was not at all flattering. He reported, for example, that the famously drunken actor John Barrymore had taken the pledge to stop drinking, and was drunk the very next night.

Most items of this type wound up in what came to be referred to as "the Monday column," for the obvious reason that it appeared on Monday. This column was arranged differently, short items separated by ellipses, or three dots. It gave the column a jazzy and urgent look. The Monday column soon became Winchell's most popular column.

Though other columnists had used gossip, Winchell became America's first true "gossip columnist." Respectable papers, and even marginally respectable papers like the *Graphic*, were often deterred from using Winchell-type items by threats of libel suits. Winchell usually avoided the problem with the clever use of slang. Using phrases like "on the verge," "this-and-that-way," and "uh-huh," all of which he invented, he was able to convey an idea without actually coming out and saying it. Winchell also used "blind items" where no names were mentioned. There might be a reference to a "well-known producer" or a "red-headed chorus girl." A typical blind item read "One of the better known moom pitcher (moving picture) execs welshed on a 100 grand roulette loss last week." Everyone knew who he was talking about, or thought they did. Still, it wasn't easy to sue, and a lawsuit usually generated even more unwelcome publicity and thus was avoided. "You want to sue me?" Winchell boasted. "Well the line forms at the right, Mister."

Winchell prowled the theaters, restaurants, and speakeasies (Prohibition was still the law of the land, though it was rarely observed in New York) with ferocious energy. Along with a few other New York columnists he not only reported Broadway he helped to create the image of Broadway as an almost mythical place. It was "The Great White Way," "The City that Never Slept." It was a world of stars and gangsters, gamblers and playboys, chorus girls and debutantes; and by reading Winchell, ordinary folk felt that they were getting a real inside look at this glamorous world. The people loved it, and he became as famous as many of those he reported on. By 1929, Winchell's column became the most popular feature in the *Graphic*. In fact, the column was just about the only thing keeping Macfadden's bizarre publication afloat.

However, Winchell was unhappy at the *Graphic* and was looking to make a move. William Randolph Hearst, who had deep pockets and was always looking to buy anyone who might expand his readership, was ready with a generous offer for Winchell to switch to his struggling New York tabloid the *Mirror*. Shortly after Winchell's departure the *Graphic* collapsed. Macfadden correctly blamed Winchell's switch for the ultimate failure of his newspaper.

Winchell and the *Mirror* were perfect for one another. His column gave the Hearst tabloid a popular and identifiable feature that resulted in a circulation boost. The *Mirror* gave Winchell a more respectable showcase. At least the paper wasn't filled with advice to the lovelorn columns and crank medical articles. Though it was every bit as sensationalist as the *Graphic* it looked more like a "regular" newspaper. It also distributed Winchell's column through King Features, the Hearst syndicate, and the column began appearing in other Hearst papers throughout the country. Walter Winchell was no longer just a New York phenomenon.

Winchell rose to fame by writing about and helping to create an image of jazz-age Broadway, the glittering "Great White Way." All that came tumbling down in the crash of 1929 and the Great Depression that followed. The Depression also marked the end of Prohibition and along with the growing popularity of films vaudeville also disappeared. Winchell adapted to the change. He began writing about "café society," a term used to describe people who were wealthy enough to go to New York's most expensive and exclusive restaurants and clubs—and who also desired publicity.

Practically every night Winchell held court in the Stork Club, a mob-financed nightclub run by an ex-bootlegger

Walter Winchell held court at New York's Stork Club. Here, he chats with Brigadier General and Mrs. Elliot Roosevelt.

from Oklahoma named Sherman Billingsley. Winchell's patronage made the Stork Club the most famous nightspot in America, probably the most famous nightspot in the whole world. Winchell sat at Table 50 while a steady stream of society folk, entertainers, politicians, and press agents tried to get his attention and curry favor with him. The column not only gave its readers what they thought was an inside look at a glittering world that they could never hope to enter personally, it also gave them the comforting feeling that the rich and famous were really no better than they were, and perhaps worse.

W. W.'s success spawned a host of gossip column rivals and imitators, but no one ever matched him in popularity or power. On the West Coast, Hollywood gossip was dominated by columnists Louella Parsons and Hedda Hopper. They became nearly as famous as Winchell, but were nowhere near as powerful. Hollywood was a one-industry town and Parsons and Hopper were really controlled by the major studios. Winchell was a law unto himself.

As Winchell's popularity grew he tried to move beyond being simply a gossip columnist to becoming a "real" journalist. At first his efforts were concentrated in the area of crime reporting. After finishing up an evening at the Stork Club or some other New York nightspot he would often join a police patrol around the city. Winchell cultivated the police in New York and elsewhere by giving them tickets to Broadway shows or other small favors. He became a regular reporter on some high-profile stories, such as the Lindbergh baby kidnapping. He was accused of actually hampering investigation of the case by leaking secret details. Winchell himself took partial credit for the apprehension of the suspect, Bruno Richard Hauptmann. He covered the trial more as a celebrity than a reporter.

What really made Walter Winchell the most popular and powerful journalist in America was radio. Television has so thoroughly dominated the lives of Americans for the last half of the twentieth century it is often forgotten how important radio once was. For many years radio was more important than newspapers, more important even than the movies. Between 1928 and 1932 the number of radio receivers in America exploded from 8 million to 18 million–and kept on growing. During that period the circulation of newspapers was dropping. Radio stars rivaled and often surpassed movie stars in popularity. During the dark days of the Great Depression, radio bound America together.

Winchell began with a weekly fifteen-minute gossip program on a local New York station in 1930. That was so popular that he was hired to emcee *The Lucky Strike Dance Hour*, a network program heard live from coast to coast. Walter Winchell introduced the various bands and did a couple of five-minute gossip spots. Here, too, he was a huge success.

But it was the Sunday night *Jergens Journal* (the sponsor was Jergens Hand Cream) that really made Winchell a national figure. It was said that you could walk down a residential street on a warm Sunday evening "never losing a word of W. W.'s broadcast as his voice came through a succession of open windows." His opening, "Good evening, Mr. and Mrs. America from border to border and coast to coast and all the ships at sea," was known to everyone.[4]

Winchell was perfect for radio. His voice was irritatingly nasal but it could not be ignored. He rattled off his commentary at such a furious staccato pace that listeners had to pay careful attention to catch what he said. Various items were punctuated with the "dot-dash" sound of a telegraph key. Winchell himself jiggled the key to set the pace of the show. Sitting in the radio studio, Winchell took off his jacket, rolled up his shirtsleeves, but never took off his trademark hat.

Like his column the radio show was a collection of celebrity gossip, sensationalism, commentary, and hard news. Radio, still a young medium, had no news tradition and newspapers fearing competition fought hard to keep news off the radio. Winchell's program provided a mixture of entertainment and news, a familiar mix on television today, but an entirely new phenomenon in 1930s radio. And more important than what he said was the fact that he said it. His introduction ran "Walter Winchell covers Broadway and Hollywood, politics and society . . . and his news of today makes the headlines of tomorrow."[5]

He usually began his programs with something sensational, like a good juicy murder. Then there was the gossip, some political stories, and international news. A movie star's rumored divorce would get the same billing and urgent delivery as a European government crisis. Broadcasts usually ended with a sentimental one-liner. Winchell, a thoroughly nasty man with few real friends and a nightmarish family life, always waxed sentimental about the virtues of friendship and family.

Winchell's power, particularly in the entertainment world, was legendary. A favorable mention in his column or on his radio show could make a career. An unfavorable mention could break one. When Winchell visited

Hollywood a dinner was given in his honor. Six hundred of the most powerful people in the movie industry showed up. A long line of speakers praised W. W. Then humorist Will Rogers rose and promised to "tell the truth." "I didn't come here to honor Mr. Winchell any more than they did. I came here for the same reason all the rest of you did . . . I was afraid not to come."

Winchell's power was recognized beyond the entertainment world. Shortly after he was elected president Franklin D. Roosevelt invited Winchell to the White House. FDR exerted his enormous charm to great effect. In less than fifteen minutes he turned the generally non-political columnist into a devoted supporter. Winchell boosted FDR at every possible opportunity.

Winchell also began to develop his relationship with another Washington figure, J. Edgar Hoover, director of the FBI. Hoover was just beginning to consolidate his power and become a real force in Washington. The two men were extremely useful to one another. Winchell regularly portrayed Hoover and his "G-men" as heroic, corruption-free supercops. Hoover secretly passed Winchell information for his column. An irony was that Winchell was also on excellent terms with many mob figures. He was granted exclusive interviews with such organized crime bosses as Al Capone and Charles "Lucky" Luciano.

In the years before World War II, Winchell was an ardent and outspoken anti-Nazi at a time when isolationism, a desire to stay out of "foreign wars" at almost any cost, was the prevailing sentiment in America. Winchell helped prepare America for the coming war, and during the war years he reached the pinnacle of his popularity. Millions tuned into his radio show for war news and for a sense of patriotic reassurance that our cause was right and we would prevail.

But when the war was over, Winchell was unable to adjust successfully to the post war world. There were many reasons for his decline. His hero Franklin Roosevelt died shortly before the end of the war. Winchell never liked FDR's successor Harry Truman, and he lost his access to the White House. Winchell's politics moved rapidly to the right, until by the 1950s he had become an outspoken backer of Joseph McCarthy, the controversial Communist-hunting senator from Wisconsin. This turnabout alienated many of Winchell's Roosevelt-era supporters.

Some of Winchell's many enemies began using the technique he had used so successfully—they dug into his past for information that would embarrass him. There was plenty to be found. One of the most embarrassing revelations was that Winchell didn't write his own material—practically everything that appeared under his byline was written by a poorly paid ghost writer named Herman Klurfeld.

But most of all it was television that brought Winchell down. Starting in the 1950s television hit America with an impact that surprised even its most enthusiastic backers. TV's greatest and most immediate impact was on network radio; television killed it. In 1959, Winchell's radio show was canceled. It had been losing its audience and sponsors for years.

Winchell was fully aware of the power of the new medium, and wanted desperately to establish himself in television. He tried a number of different formats including an attempt to recreate his radio show on television. Still wearing his hat in an era when hats were no longer being worn, and acting like what one critic called "a nervous elf," the whole enterprise looked dated and the show failed to attract viewers. In the end he achieved his greatest television success as the narrator of crime shows like "The Untouchables," which dramatized FBI cases from the 1920s and 1930s. The appeal was no longer the latest hot scoop, but pure nostalgia.

The popular and sharp-tongued TV host Jack Parr derided Winchell as "a silly old man." It was the sort of remark that no performer would have dared to make during Winchell's glory days. Yet in the late 1950s, Parr prospered and Winchell didn't.[6]

Television also had a tremendous impact on newspapers. The decline in newspaper readership and influence that began with radio accelerated with television. The once-mighty Hearst chain crumbled. On October 16, 1963, the *New York Mirror*, which had been losing circulation, advertising, and money for a long time, shut down for good. The Winchell column was switched to other New York Hearst papers, but it was smaller and more heavily edited. These papers, too, were in trouble. By 1967 the Hearst corporation refused to renew Winchell's contract–and his long- running column, which had been on life support for some years, expired.

Winchell died in 1972. His daughter, Walda, was the only mourner at his funeral. A memorial service held a few weeks later attracted only 150, and most of them drifted out before the service was over. He no longer inspired fear or respect or even hatred. Many people reading his obituary were surprised to discover that he had not died a long time ago.

Though Winchell was forgotten, his influence is still with us. The mixture of celebrity gossip and hard news, which he more than anyone else in America popularized, is so much a part of the media today we barely notice it anymore.

"If one surveys this culture of Monica Lewinsky and O. J. Simpson and constant gossip and salaciousness, and one tries to trace the roots you find yourself at Walter Winchell," said Winchell biographer Neal Gabler. "He was not only present at the creation of this modern journalism but in many respects he was the creation."[7]

5
DEAD!

On the evening of March 19, 1927, the police found the body of Albert Snyder in the bedroom of his home in Queens, New York. His head had been smashed by blows from a lead window sash weight.

His wife, Ruth, told police a confused tale of intruders breaking into the house, but they didn't believe her. She quickly broke down and confessed that the murderer was her lover Judd Gray. Gray was arrested and also confessed, but blamed everything on Ruth.

It was a tawdry, inept, and essentially commonplace and uninteresting murder. Journalist Damon Runyon dubbed the killing the "Dumb-bell murder" because "it was so dumb." Yet since it was essentially about sex it was of great interest to New York newspapermen of the time, the era that was called Jazz Age Journalism. New York papers reported every tidbit of the trial, including dreadful self-serving poems written by Ruth Snyder herself. During the trial Ruth received 167 oddball offers of marriage.

The outcome of the trial was never in doubt. Both were convicted and sentenced to die in the electric chair.

The sentences were carried out on the night of January 12, 1928.

If the story ended there this case, like so many other once-sensational murders, would probably be forgotten. But something else happened.

As was customary reporters had been invited to witness the execution. One of the reporters, Tom Howard of the New York *Daily News*, defied prison regulations and strapped a small camera to his leg. A trip line, concealed under his clothes, ran up his leg and body to his wrist. Just as the executioner threw the switch sending a lethal current into Ruth Snyder's body Howard lifted his trouser leg, squeezed the plunger in his hand and snapped a photo of Snyder's body as the current shot through it. This photo (which was very fuzzy and heavily retouched) took up the entire front page of the *News* the next day. The headline screamed "**DEAD!**" Without any pun intended it was the single most shocking photo that had ever been published in a newspaper anywhere. It has given the Snyder-Gray case a sort of immortality it does not deserve. The photo is a monument to journalistic bad taste, but also a monument to the power of photography.

Other New York tabloids had covered the Snyder-Gray case as closely as the *News*. After Ruth Snyder's execution the *Graphic* told its readers:

"Don't fail to read tomorrow's *Graphic*. An installment that thrills and stuns! A story that fairly pierces the heart and reveals Ruth Snyder's last thoughts on earth; that pulses the blood as it discloses her final letters. Think of it! A woman's final thoughts just before she is clutched in the deadly snare that sears and burns and **FRIES AND KILLS!** Her very last words! Exclusively in tomorrow's *Graphic*."[1]

The most shocking photo ever published: Ruth Snyder after being killed by the electric chair in 1928.

But "her very last words," if that is indeed what the *Graphic* actually printed, couldn't match the photograph. The *News* sold 250,000 extra copies, and then had to run off 750,000 additional copies later. The second time the headline read, **FUNERALS HELD** For Gray, Mrs. Snyder. Such was the selling power of a sensational photo.

Photography was developed in the 1830s and 1840s. By the 1860s it had become quite sophisticated. Mathew Brady's photographs of the American Civil War remain some of the most striking images ever captured. Though Brady's equipment seems clumsy and primitive by modern standards the results were amazing. There was, however, no way of reproducing photographs in newspapers or magazines.

That doesn't mean that mid-nineteenth-century publications were without illustrations. Drawings usually engraved by hand on wooden blocks had been used in American newspapers, though until the Civil War they were not very common. Weekly or monthly magazines made better use of these engravings because they had more time to spend on engraving and printing. Some of the illustrations they used were superb.

The use of illustrations in American publications increased dramatically during the Civil War. Artists sometimes used photographs by Brady or other photographers as the basis for the drawings and engravings that were used in newspapers and magazines. By 1891 it is estimated that there were over a thousand artists at work in the country supplying illustrations for five thousand newspapers and magazines. But a drawing, even if it was skillfully done and based on a photograph, was not the same as a photograph itself, and hand-cutting woodblocks was still time-consuming and expensive.

By the 1890s a variety of methods for producing an engraving that could be used in a newspaper directly from a photograph had been developed. In 1893, Stephen Horgan, the art editor of the New York *Herald*, suggested to its owner, James Gordon Bennett, that halftones made from photographs could be printed in the newspaper. Bennett consulted his pressmen, who told him the idea was preposterous. The imperious Bennett promptly fired Horgan.

By the time of the Spanish-American War (1898) both artists and photographers, as well as reporters, were sent out to cover the news. Big city newspapers began to employ photographers who carried their heavy, awkward equipment and their flashlight powder to all sorts of assignments. Still, many veteran newspapermen scorned the new technique and denounced photos in newspapers as a terrible waste of space.

It was the yellow journalists like William Randolph Hearst who first really appreciated the power of a photograph in a newspaper. Hearst himself was an enthusiastic amateur photographer and he personally covered the Spanish-American War as a journalist and a photographer.

No newspaper in America was ever as fully identified with photographs as the New York *Daily News*. And as with the photo of the execution of Ruth Snyder, these photos tended to be highly sensational.

The *Daily News*, or the *Illustrated Daily News* as it was first called, was the creation of Captain Joseph Medill Patterson, one of the grandsons of Joseph Medill, founder of the *Chicago Tribune*. For a time Patterson was copublisher of the *Tribune* with his cousin Colonel Robert McCormick. The arrangement had never been a comfortable one, because the two men were so different in personality and outlook. McCormick was a hidebound reactionary; Patterson, at least in his younger days, was thought of as a socialist by others of his wealthy class.

Captain Patterson had been inspired by the success of the *Daily Mirror* in London. He became well acquainted with British journalism during his service in London during World War I. The *Mirror* had been started in 1903 as a newspaper for women but was soon converted into a "halfpenny illustrated." It was half the size of a standard newspaper—tabloid size—and was sensational, breezy, and most of all full of pictures. In two years the *Daily Mirror* was selling half a million copies in London, and pulling in enormous profits. The tabloid size had been used in America before, but it was only after the great success of the English tabloids that it became a popular size for newspapers in America.

The tabloid size also became synonymous with sensationalized newspapers, and tabloid journalism came to mean what yellow journalism had meant in an earlier era.

Colonel McCormick agreed to put some of the family fortune into founding an illustrated tabloid in New York. Perhaps he thought it would be a good investment. Perhaps he just wanted to get his cousin out of Chicago so he could have the *Tribune* for himself. Whatever the reason it ultimately proved to be a very good investment indeed.

The *Illustrated Daily News* made its debut on June 19, 1919. Half the front page was taken up with a picture of the Prince of Wales (later and very briefly King Edward

DAILY NEWS

Average net paid circulation of THE NEWS, July, 1926.
Sunday 1,194,042
Daily - 1,054,752

NEW YORK'S PICTURE NEWSPAPER

FINAL EDITION

Vol. 8. No. 52. 32 Pages   New York, Wednesday, August 25, 1926   2 Cents

FANS RIOT AS RUDY RESTS

Story on Page 3

The appeal of the *Daily News* was the photos.
Here, actor Rudolph Valentino in an open casket.

VII and then after his abdication the Duke of Windsor). The prince was about to visit America and presumably had set the hearts of American womanhood fluttering. The popular and inexplicable American obsession with British royalty persists to this day. The *News* had a promotional gimmick to add to the general interest in royalty—it sponsored a beauty contest. In ads in *The New York Times* and other papers the *News* announced **SEE NEW YORK'S MOST BEAUTIFUL GIRLS EVERY MORNING IN THE ILLUS-TRATED DAILY NEWS**. There were, of course, photos of all the contestants.[2]

Despite the gimmicks, however, the *News* was not an immediate success. Its initial circulation of 200,000 dropped to an anemic 26,000 in the second month. Two of the paper's four reporters were fired. Patterson then discovered that the largest pool of potential readers for his new paper was not among those who already read English-language papers, but among the masses of immigrants whose command of English was limited and poorly educated Americans who previously read no other newspaper. It was the pictures, and not the words, that would sell the paper. The *News* was put on stands that had previously sold only foreign-language papers.

Patterson hung around newsstands to see what people were reading in his paper. The new comic strips seemed to attract a lot of attention, and the readers favored crime news and sports stories. Subway riders liked the tabloid size because it was easier to handle while riding in the crowded cars. By 1924 the *Daily News* circulation of 750,000 was the largest in the country. By 1929 the figure was 1,320,000, gains that took place while the circulations of other New York papers stood still or declined. Just before World War II, *Daily News* circulation hit the two million mark, making it by far the most popular newspaper in the country. And it was the pictures—dramatic enough to make the potential reader stop, look again, and buy—that made the paper the success it became. All newspapers, particularly the tabloids, relied increasingly on photos to grab and hold customers. But no paper ever did it as well as the *News* in its glory days.

If the New York *Daily News* was the symbol of sensationalized photojournalism the photographer who symbolized the era was a pudgy, round-faced, cigar-chomping character known as Weegee. His real name was Arthur Fellig, an Austrian immigrant who worked as a freelance photographer in New York during the 1930s and 1940s. When he began his career, Weegee's stock and trade was taking pictures of violent crimes and horrible accidents for the New York tabloids.

Weegee lived in a cluttered one-room apartment across the street from police headquarters. The police shortwave radio in his apartment was on twenty-four hours a day. One picture editor who knew him said, "Even in slumber he is responsive to [the police radio]. He will sleep through fifteen unpromising police calls and leap out of bed at the promising sixteenth."

When he wasn't sleeping or working on a job, he cruised the city in a 1938 Chevrolet, also equipped with a police shortwave radio. He always used a Speed Graphic camera, a large, heavy cube-shaped device with a flashbulb reflector mounted on the side. The Speed Graphic was cumbersome and slow by modern standards. The photographer could only take one shot at a time. But it took marvelously clear photos, and it was the standard equipment for news photographers everywhere, even well into the 1950s, when smaller, lighter, and faster equipment was already available. Like the reporter's snap-brim fedora, the Speed Graphic had become a symbol of the news photographer's profession.

Weegee had the reputation of always being the first photographer on the scene of a murder or grisly accident. He was so good at being the man on the spot that picture editors joked he got his advance information from a Ouija Board, the device that is supposed to spell out messages from the spirit world. That's how he got his nickname "Weegee." Like other photographers of the time Weegee never hesitated to "improve" a shot. He would often rearrange the position of a corpse to make it look more dramatic or artistic.

Of murders Weegee wrote, "People get bumped off . . . on the sidewalks of New York. The only thing unusual about these killings is that they are never solved. The guys are always neatly dressed . . . fall face up . . . with their pearl gray hats along side of them. Some day I'll follow one of those guys with a 'pearl gray hat,' have my camera all set and get the actual killing . . . could be . . ."[3]

At the start of his career Weegee's work appeared primarily in the *News* and other New York tabloids. His images could catch the eye, even on a crowded newsstand. But it wasn't just the tabloids that wanted pictures of this type, they began selling to more upscale publications like *Life* magazine. In a collection of his photos Weegee reproduced a statement that was attached to a check from *Life*. It read, "TWO MURDERS 35.00. One of the photos cost twenty-five dollars. The other picture they bought was only a cheap murder, with not many bullets . . . so they paid ten dollars for that."

This is the type of photo Weegee lived for: A man lies dead in the doorway of his cafe and none of the neighbors hanging out the windows know anything about it.

In 1945, Weegee put some of his best photographs together in a book called *Naked City*. "Then something happened," he wrote. "There was a sudden drop in Murders and Fires (my two best sellers, my bread and butter). I couldn't understand that. With so many millions of people, it just wasn't normal, but it did give me a chance to look over the pictures I had been accumulating."[4] His tough-guy prose was nearly as good as his photographs.

The book was a huge success and made a celebrity out of the tabloid news photographer. He shut off his police radio for good and began photographing celebrities like Marilyn Monroe and John F. Kennedy. Today Weegee's photos, once considered pure tabloid trash, are part of the permanent collection of The Museum of Modern Art.

An interest, indeed very nearly an obsession, with celebrities began to become a regular part of the press during the 1920s. People such as Babe Ruth, Charles Lindbergh, and English Channel swimmer Gertrude Ederle became popular press favorites. In late August 1926, Charles Eliot, the former president of Harvard, and movie star Rudolph Valentino both died. The *News* devoted six pages of text and photos to Valentino and one paragraph to Eliot. Though the tabloid press may have been extreme, even the respectable press gave Valentino a lot more space. At the time critics were outraged. Today this sort of balance would be considered normal.

Celebrity photos, of course, became a standby for the tabloids. At first these were generally studio publicity shots or other carefully posed pictures. But the development of new lighter and faster cameras led to the media phenomenon we call the paparazzi.

The word comes from an influential 1960 Italian film *La Dolce Vita* directed by Federico Fellini. It's a film about celebrities and journalists. One of the characters is a celebrity-chasing photographer named Paparazzo who ultimately gave his name to the whole profession. The character was based on a real person, who now is know as "Mr. Paparazzo."

The relationship between celebrities and journalists, particularly entertainment celebrities, is often an ambiguous one. Movie stars, pop music stars, and others depend on publicity to keep their names and faces in front of the public. But standard publicity-type shots of the individual smiling and waving at the camera are of little interest—they are quite literally a dime a dozen. The pictures that now command high fees are those that the celebrity does not want taken—the actress who has gained 40 pounds, and looks it; the rock star who has been arrested for drug possession and is being hauled into court; the celebrated couple glaring angrily at one another as they leave the divorce court. And there are some famous people or people who become famous briefly who just don't want to have their pictures taken at all.

There are a relatively small number of famous individuals who are regularly followed by paparazzi, just waiting to get that one embarrassing or revealing shot. There is a whole subcategory of photos showing angry celebrities attacking the paparazzi who are trailing them. These photos, taken by other paparazzi, often command very high prices. Photographers have been known to deliberately provoke their subjects in order to get an angry shot.

One of the more striking examples of life imitating art is that the voluptuous Swedish actress Anita Ekberg, a star of the Fellini film, became a favorite target of the paparazzi. While she generally welcomed publicity, sometimes it was more than she wanted. One night in October 1960, Ekberg stormed out of her Roman villa carrying a bow and arrow. She managed to wound one of the crowd of photographers who had been pursuing her. Nobody got a picture of that, but one paparazzo, Marcello Geppetti, did get a celebrated shot of Ekberg kicking one of his colleagues.[5]

Frank Sinatra would often sic his burly bodyguards on the photographers, while other stars, like the short-tempered American actor Sean Penn, have thrown the punches themselves. All of this is duly recorded in the tabloids.

Today's paparazzi have long-distance telephoto lenses and night scopes, and have been known to hire helicopters. So celebrities can be under the photographers' surveillance even if they don't know it.

No one in the entertainment business can honestly claim they are publicity shy. It is, rather, the sort of publicity they get that they are sensitive about. However, for many years the chief target of paparazzi and celebrity-hunting journalists in general was Jacqueline Kennedy, who in large part shied away from publicity. This was particularly true after President John Kennedy's assassination and her subsequent marriage to the wealthy Aristotle Onassis. Jackie Onassis was, in fact, an intensely private person. On the rare occasions she sought publicity, it was in connection with some public project she was interested in, but she could hardly take a step out in public without attracting a mob of photographers. She even sued one particularly aggressive photographer, but as long as the public seemed to have a consuming interest in absolutely everything she did, even if she wasn't doing anything very interesting, the paparazzi dogged her footsteps.

Even the long-running interest in "Jackie" pales before the virtual obsession with Princess Diana of Britain. The obsession began with the "fairy tale" marriage of "Princess Di" to Prince Charles, heir apparent to the British throne. At first the press coverage was romantic, respectful, almost worshipful. But the obsession increased as the "fairy tale" began to unravel, finally ending in a messy divorce. For years the princess was the most famous woman in the world, and undoubtedly the most photographed person in history. The fascination with the princess is perhaps most natural in Britain. Britain is also the birthplace of the modern tabloid press, and remains the trendsetter in that dubious field. Many of the editors and reporters of the U.S. sensationalist press and what has been called "tabloid television" are British and got their start on London's Fleet Street, traditional home of the British press. As has already been noted, Americans have had a long-term fascination with the British royal family. The trials and tribulations of this dysfunctional royal family receives almost as much attention in America as in Britain itself.

When Italian paparazzo Mario Brenna got a fuzzy telephoto picture of Princess Di kissing her new boyfriend Dodi al Fayed on a beach in Sardinia he was paid more than $650,000. It was a good investment for the three British tabloids that used the photos. Circulations jumped by 750,000 each. The photos also sold to American supermarket tabloids, where they proved to be great circulation boosters. For sixteen years, photos of Princess Di

Over the years, the media coverage of Princess Diana changed. As her popularity soared, the photographers would do anything to capture any image of her—happy, sad, private, or public.

had been circulation boosters, not only for the supermarket tabloids but for magazines like *People*. She was always the most popular cover subject of that publication, of many of the women's magazines, and even of news magazines like *Time* and *Newsweek*.

When, on August 31, 1997, Princess Di, Dodi Fayed, and their driver were killed in a crash in a Paris tunnel, it became an event that eclipsed everything else in the news, not only in the tabloids but in much of the mainstream press as well. Mother Teresa died that same week, and while her death did not go unnoticed, it was completely overshadowed by the Princess Di tragedy.

What makes this accident particularly significant for us is that the photographers, the paparazzi themselves, not only covered the story, they became a central part of it. As always the princess was surrounded by a pack of photographers, but during her August visit to Paris interest was at an unusually high pitch because she was with her new boyfriend, and there were rumors of marriage.

When the Mercedes 280 carrying Princess Di and Dodi sped into the Paris tunnel it was being pursued by a group of paparazzi on motor scooters. Within minutes of the accident there were a dozen or more photographers hovering vulturelike around the scene taking pictures. As news of the deadly crash spread, the pursuing photographers were immediately blamed for causing the crash, and for hindering rescue efforts. Several paparazzi were arrested. The Princess's brother Charles Spencer publicly proclaimed that "blood is on all the hands" of every publisher and editor "that has paid for intrusive and exploitative photographs of her . . ." The public seemed to agree.

After a long and exhaustive investigation French authorities concluded that the photographers did not cause the accident. It is doubtful that the French report, no matter how thorough, will answer all questions or satisfy everyone. But facts have emerged that blur the image of a harassed and frightened princess pursued to her death by bloodthirsty photographers. The driver of the Mercedes, an employee of Dodi al Fayed's millionaire father, was drunk and driving at an extremely high speed. The tunnel in which the accident occurred was badly designed and had been the scene of many accidents. The Mercedes in which Princess Di was riding was an armored vehicle, and she was in absolutely no danger from photographers on motor scooters. She couldn't even be seen through the heavily tinted windows. While the photographers may have been a nuisance they were no real danger and there was no reason to drive at breakneck speeds to get away from them.

Still, there was a good deal of public soul-searching from the media. Tabloids announced that they would not print photos of the dying princess trapped inside her car after the accident—though such photos existed. Some sensationalist publications like the *National Enquirer* said that they would have nothing to do with the more ruthless breed of photographer, though they had regularly used the photographs of such paparazzi in the past. Celebrities and some politicians promised to push for stricter privacy laws that would limit the activities of the more aggressive photographers. It is far from clear, however, whether such laws would be constitutional or could be effectively enforced in the United States. Britain, which does not have the sort of constitutional guarantees of press freedom that exist in the United States and also has a new Protection From Harassment Act, is still the home of some of the world's most sensationalist and successful tabloids. Legal limits on the British tabloids have never worked well. There is no reason to believe that they would be any more effective in the United States.

In fact, after the initial outburst of public indignation and media self-criticism following the death of Princess Di, little seems to have really changed. One photographer, who does not deal in paparazzi-type photos, noted cynically that the demand for her type of legitimate news photography had actually declined. "It all goes back to demand, what the public wants. They're not interested in the real world. They want to see this dream world of celebrities and royals."[6]

Captain Patterson of the New York *Illustrated Daily News* surely would have understood that.

6

LIVE!!

Before television there was the newsreel. The American newsreel was a ten-minute potpourri of motion picture footage released twice a week to motion picture theaters throughout the country.

For more than half a century, from 1911 to 1967, the newsreel remained virtually unchanged. Newsreels were predictably a part of every theater's program like the cartoon and the coming attractions.

Newsreels were never as important as newspapers or even radio news. But most people in America went to the movies regularly, at least once a week. Newsreels were a part of their lives and helped to shape the way in which they saw the world before the advent of television. Most Americans saw World War II through the newsreels.

Newsreels were never as sensationalist as the tabloids. They didn't have to grab peoples' attention to get an audience. The newsreel already had a captive audience that had come to see the feature film, or perhaps a double feature. The movie audience was also a "family audience," everybody, mom, dad, and the kids, went to the movies.

If any segment of the audience was offended or frightened by what they saw that would be bad for business. Though crime and disasters were regular parts of the newsreel there were few Weegee-type scenes of the bloody, bullet-riddled body on the street.

Faking newsreel footage, particularly in the early days, was commonplace. Footage of everything from the coronation of Edward VII to battlefield scenes from World War I was faked and passed off as real to an audience that was quite unsophisticated about photography

An interesting variation on war coverage came in 1914 when the Mutual Film Company bought the "rights" to the Mexican revolution. For $25,000 and a 50 percent share of the earnings, General Pancho Villa guaranteed not to "allow any other moving picture men except those of the company in which he is interested on the field during his battles." The contract specified that, wherever possible, battles would be held during daylight hours and at times convenient for the Mutual cameramen.[1]

"Re-creations" of newsworthy events was a common practice. Some newsreel producers claimed that the re-creation was often better than the "real thing." They insisted that newsreel cameramen had the same right as print reporters in re-creating the event. Of course, the viewer was not told that what was being shown was a re-creation and not the real thing.

More significant than the faking, and the strange purchase of rights to a war, was the essentially frivolous nature of newsreels. Newsreels were regarded primarily as part of the entertainment provided by the motion picture theater. The average ten-minute reel contained coverage of a beauty contest, or a pie-eating contest, or a strongman who could pull a locomotive with his teeth, or the marriage of one pair of identical twins to another. It was the same sort of "human interest story" that the tabloids used, but this was something the newsreels did better. Newsreels also loved celebrities. They doted on people like the aviator Charles Lindbergh, the Dionne quintuplets, Babe Ruth, and of course the British royal family.

But most of all newsreels loved movie stars. This is hardly surprising since many of the companies that made newsreels also made the motion pictures being shown in theaters that the companies also owned. There was no nasty Hollywood gossip in the newsreels, just happy shots of Mary Pickford at home or Clark Gable on location.

A lot of the techniques first developed by newsreel cameramen were later used by television cameramen. And it was television that ultimately made newsreels irrelevant and ended their long popularity. The last newsreel was released on December 26, 1967. By that time most theaters had already stopped showing them.

Today we can see that television has dominated the second half of the twentieth century. But in the years following World War II, when television was just beginning to become available to the public, its potential was often underestimated.

In 1946, Darryl Zanuck, head of 20th Century-Fox, said, "Television won't be able to hold on to any market it captures after the first six months. People will soon get tired of staring at a plywood box every night."

That is a statement that ranks high on anybody's list of bad predictions.

The news impact of television was underestimated for an even longer period. In the 1960 election, candidate

John F. Kennedy was convinced it was the big newsmagazines like *Time* and *Newsweek* that would have a critical impact on the election. His attitude toward a scheduled televised debate with Richard Nixon was almost casual. Yet we now know that it was Kennedy's cool and articulate television performance that swung the momentum of the election in his direction.

The sensationalism that had been part of newspapers for so long was not a part of early television news for a variety of reasons. Television was, and to a great extent still is, primarily an entertainment medium. While it was a sensational headline or photo that made many readers buy a newspaper off the newsstand, it was the entertainment that made viewers choose one television station over another. There wasn't a lot of news on early television—up until 1962 national news shows were only fifteen minutes a day. Most local news shows were the same. The broadcast of news was regarded as more of a public service than as an essential part of the television business.

In theory, anybody can start a newspaper. But in the early days of television there were only a very limited number of broadcast channels available, and these were licensed by the government. Because of this the government can and does impose certain controls and standards on broadcasters. Even in the 1960s many large cities still only had eight or ten channels, and these were dominated by the three major television networks.

Television was also regarded as a "family medium." It was broadcast "right into your living room." Material that might be deemed offensive or harmful to children simply was not shown. If someone wanted to know the details of a sex scandal or gruesome murder he could always read

The first televised debate between presidential candidates Kennedy and Nixon helped swing the 1960 election. Politics would never be the same.

Edward R. Murrow was one of the most respected journalists to ever work in television.

one of the tabloids. Government regulators might punish a broadcaster whose news programs were too graphic or sensationalized–though the government rarely did. A far more effective restraint was exercised by advertisers. Major companies did not want to be associated with programs that were regarded as sleazy.

Early television news shows tended to be straightforward and sober. Early news documentaries typically tried to deal with serious subjects, and some like Edward R. Murrow's "Harvest of Shame," which revealed the plight of migrant farm workers in America were well researched, extremely powerful, and sparked changes in national policy. Such programs, however, rarely attracted a large audience. News documentaries may have won prizes and praise, but they didn't bring in the profits and were a low priority for network television.

The technology of television expanded rapidly from the 1950s on. It went from black and white to color, from local broadcasts to national broadcasts, from an eight- or ten-hour broadcast day to around-the-clock transmission. Then in the 1960s satellites allowed the transmission of television broadcasts around the world. There was an enormous expansion in the number of channels available, first broadcast channels and increasingly channels available by cable and satellite. In the 1960s an average viewer might be able to chose only from a half-dozen channels. By the 1990s that same viewer could have a choice of ninety or more channels.

The economics of television news also changed. News, particularly local news, became profitable. With a larger number of channels available there was increased competition among news shows for viewers. Local news began to concentrate more and more on those stories that had traditionally brought readers to newspapers: crime, disasters, scandals, and that whole range of "soft news" that is lumped under the heading of human interest stories. But even though the emphasis had changed, regular television news rarely reached the level of true tabloid journalism—at least until the late 1980s.

Programs like "Hard Copy" and "A Current Affair," which became extremely popular during the late 1980s and early 1990s, were true tabloid television. They were not the products of the news department of any network or station—they were independently produced and syndicated to the highest bidder. These shows concentrated primarily on crime, celebrity scandal and gossip, and other sensational topics. Like the supermarket tabloids, these TV shows were willing to pay for interviews or other information, which is something no respectable journalist in America is ever supposed to do.

There was a flood of poorly researched and one-sided "documentaries" on sensational topics like UFOs and Satanism. The line between "entertainment" and news became blurred. Programs like "Unsolved Mysteries" would present "re-creations" of real events, usually crimes. Though such presentations were labeled as re-creations, the casual viewer might easily become confused. There was also a vogue for "docudramas," made-for-television movies that were supposed to be based on real current events, everything from the Branch Davidian tragedy at Waco to the breakup of the marriage of Prince Charles and Princess Diana. These shows were highly fictionalized in order to make them more dramatically satisfying. However, they were promoted as being "ripped from today's headlines" and once again it was not difficult for the viewer to become confused about what was real and what was created. This sort of television almost always drew much larger audiences than standard news shows.

A symbol of sensationalism in TV news is Geraldo Rivera. In the 1970s he was a popular and flamboyant on-camera journalist for ABC in New York. He won awards for such groundbreaking investigative reports as his 1972 exposé of the terrible conditions children lived in at Willowbrook, a mental hospital in Staten Island. His reports led to real reforms at this institution and others like it.

But after he left ABC he embarked on syndicated shows that, while popular, were clearly more sensationalism than journalism. In 1986 there was a tremendous buildup for a show on which Rivera was supposed to blast through the walls of Al Capone's alleged vault (actually an abandoned tunnel beneath a hotel that had once been the gangster's headquarters) live on national television. The show drew a tremendous audience but turned out to be an embarrassing flop because the "vault" contained absolutely nothing of interest. Rivera-produced specials on "Devil Worship" were very popular, though they were pure sensationalism and were as empty of real content as Al Capone's "vault."[2]

Geraldo became host of a popular syndicated talk show. Topics discussed ranged from the purely sensational, like "girl gangs," to the serious, like race relations. In 1988, during the taping of one show, a fight broke out between Roy Innis, the chairman of the Congress of Racial Equality, and a group of neo-Nazis in the audience. During the brawl Rivera was hit in the nose with a chair. Rivera knew full well that a fight was likely and being hit with a chair got him and his show a great deal of publicity.

In 1994, Rivera went over to CNBC, an all-news cable channel owned by the NBC network. His new show was called "Rivera Live" and was supposed to be a nightly discussion primarily of legal issues. Rivera had originally been trained as a lawyer. The show immediately plunged into a nightly discussion of the highly sensational O. J. Simpson murder trial, and Rivera announced his intention of making his show "the program of record" on the trial. "Rivera Live" was almost exclusively O. J. for over a year and proved to be very popular, drawing the highest ratings CNBC ever had.

After the O. J. trials ended, Rivera went on to other high-profile crimes and then to almost full-time coverage of the impeachment trial of President Clinton. The show has been so successful that Rivera gave up his syndicated daytime show and has taken on straight news duties at CNBC, including a new show "Upfront Tonight." He has also announced his desire to become anchor on the NBC nightly news–a prospect that many professional television journalists find distasteful and embarrassing.

Today a great many Americans get most of their news through television, and there is more news than ever on television. There are now several national all-news channels and an explosion of newsmagazine shows on the networks. The news isn't necessarily any better or more informative. There is just a lot more of it. The more competition the greater the tendency to use sensationalism to pull in the audience. Today even network news shows regularly deal with topics that would not have been touched in an earlier era.

Television can do something that no other medium can even approach: It can present a news event live—as it happens.

Newspaper reporters interpreted events in words; newsreels and news photos could be edited or simply not used. Even a live radio report was not the same, because the reporter had to describe what was happening. But live television coverage of a news event is unpredictable and reporters and editors sometimes have little control over what the viewer might see.

People who read a newspaper account of the Kennedy-Nixon debates, or even heard them live on the radio, had a very different impression from those who saw the debate on television. It wasn't so much what the candidates said, but the way they looked and moved that made all the difference.

One of the most dramatic early examples of an utterly unpredictable news event happening live on television took place in connection with the assassination of President Kennedy. The assassination itself was not seen live, though TV cameras were on the scene quickly. Two days after the assassination suspect Lee Harvey Oswald was being led past live TV cameras in the basement of Dallas police headquarters when a man rushed out of the crowd and shot him. This was shown on live television. It was an unpredictable, shocking, sensational, and utterly unforgettable moment for all who saw it.

Live television has brought both triumph and tragedy into the home. Television brought live pictures of Neil Armstrong's first steps on the moon in 1969. Later it broadcast live the explosion of the space shuttle *Challenger*.

Lee Harvey Oswald walks into Dallas police headquarters minutes before being shot on live television.

Man walks on the moon!

Increasingly, however, live television has been used for purely sensationalistic purposes. Many large television news departments have camera-equipped helicopters. These are used mainly to track automobile traffic during rush-hour traffic reports. They are also used to cover high-speed police chases, large fires, and sometimes to hover over crime scenes. Usually such events attract a huge audience.

In May 1998 a man stopped his pickup truck in the middle of a Los Angeles freeway to stage an impromptu demonstration. While choppers for Los Angeles TV stations hovered overhead the man set his truck on fire, then took a shotgun, put it to his head, and pulled the trigger. The suicide was seen live by hundreds of thousands of fascinated and horrified viewers. The bloody end to the drama was unanticipated, but still news directors could have predicted what was going to happen and pulled away before the final shot was fired. A couple of stations actually did. Most did not, though after they were inundated with complaints, the stations issued a variety of excuses and apologies.[3] If William Randolph Hearst had possessed the technology he would certainly have shown the suicide live, though he probably wouldn't have bothered with an apology afterward.

The ratings for this live on-the-air suicide were terrific, and there is no reason to believe that most stations won't act exactly the same way if the opportunity arises.

An entirely new and unpredictable element has been added to the story of sensationalist journalism with the growth of the Internet.

Almost no one can afford to start a television or even radio station. Very few can afford to start a newspaper or national magazine. But practically anyone with a personal computer and a small amount of technical knowledge can start a Web site, and hundreds of thousands have.

There are Web sites for virtually any area of interest no matter how obscure and for any cause no matter how nutty or vile. Most of the Web sites are visited only by a limited and like-minded audience, but occasionally someone breaks out of the pack.

The premier example of this is the aptly named Matt Drudge. Drudge was a self-proclaimed failure. He finished number 325 in his high school class of 350. In 1994 his father bought him a computer in the hopes that he might do something with his life. As it turned out, he did. Drudge had been working in the CBS Studio's gift shop in Hollywood, and he listened to gossip and searched the dumpsters for information that he would post on his Web site called "the Drudge Report." Most of his information was low-level Hollywood gossip and he didn't attract much attention until he turned to politics.[4]

In January 1998, Drudge heard that *Newsweek* had been working on a story about a sexual relationship between President Bill Clinton and a twenty-one-year-old White House intern named Monica Lewinsky. Actually a lot of people, including journalists, investigators for special prosecutor Kenneth Starr, and just about every political insider in Washington, had already heard about Monica Lewinsky. But Drudge was the first to put the story out in public. And within days virtually everyone in America had seen or heard of the story.

Newsweek editors had postponed publishing the Lewinsky story. Drudge didn't have any editors to satisfy, and no weekly publishing schedule to adhere to. He could just type it into his computer and instantly lots of people would know.

The Lewinsky story made Drudge famous (or infamous) and people began sending their rumors, tips, and gossip to him—and a lot of it wound up in his report on the Net. Many of Drudge's items are unsubstantiated and some have been shown to be downright false. He is currently being sued for at least one report. But unlike a television station or a newspaper, Drudge and other Internet "journalists" have little to lose either financially or in reputation. The more he is denounced and sued the more popular Matt Drudge seems to become. In July 1998 the Drudge Report pulled in 10 million hits according to World 1000, which monitors independent Web sites.

Drudge's notoriety even earned him a weekly half-hour show on the Fox News Channel. He clearly patterns himself after the godfather of gossip columnists Walter Winchell. Drudge always wears a Winchell-type fedora, and the fedora along with an old manual typewriter are the symbols of his TV show. But he lacks Winchell's staccato voice and hyperactive, aggressive personality. He comes across as a rather bland, almost apologetic figure. Whether Drudge will ever approach his journalistic idol in popularity and influence is an open question.

"I think it's a natural extension of a new media in which to publish," says Joshua Fouts, managing editor of *Online Journalism Review*, a site hosted and partly funded by the Annenberg School for Communication at the University of Southern California. "What online journalism does is it takes us back to the

Matt Drudge prepares for his first television show, adopting a Walter Winchell-style persona.

very beginnings of journalism, almost to the era when free speech and free press began. In those eras the printers were the journalists." Some of the first publishers dealt in gossip, says Fouts, and it still exists. "The fact that the *Enquirer* and the *Star* [supermarket tabloids] outsell any of the large metro dailies speaks volumes of what the public wants."

George Kennedy, a professor of journalism at the Missouri School of Journalism in Columbia, Missouri, agrees. "It's one of the delights of the new electronic age," he says.[5]

Whether it is really a delight to be taken back to the days of the New York *Sun* and other representatives of the penny press is a proposition that can be debated. But there seems to be no doubt that the Drudge type of online journalistic gossip and sensationalism is here to stay—at least for a while.

7

THE TRIAL OF THE CENTURY

There is nothing quite like a good juicy trial, particularly one involving any combination of sex, celebrity, and murder, to drive up circulation or ratings and set the pulse of the true yellow journalist (and the public) racing. Sometimes it is the press or the media itself that becomes the most important part of the story. The history of sensational journalism in America can be traced by looking at a few "Trials of the Century."

THE HALL-MILLS CASE

On September 16, 1922, a gruesome discovery was made on a quiet country lane outside of New Brunswick, New Jersey. The bodies of a man and woman lay under a crab apple tree in perfectly composed, almost lifelike poses. The man was wearing a dark blue suit and clerical collar. His expensive Panama hat had been carefully placed over his head, as if to shield him from the heat.

One of the man's arms was wrapped around the body of a woman wearing a bright blue and red polka-dot dress.

Her legs were crossed and the hem of her skirt was modestly pulled down below the knees as far as the material would reach. Her face was covered by a scarf.

The gruesome violence of the scene was not obvious at first. But when the man's hat was removed it revealed he had been shot through the head. Beneath the scarf it could be seen that the woman had also been shot in the head, and her throat had been slashed and mutilated.

Propped up against the dead man's shoe, almost like an identification label in a museum, was a calling card. It identified him as the Reverend Edward Wheeler Hall, pastor of the wealthiest and most respected Episcopalian church in New Brunswick.

The woman had not been labeled but her identity was quickly established. She was Mrs. Eleanor Mills, wife of the church janitor and a mainstay of the congregation's choir. Reverend Hall was forty-one; Mrs. Mills thirty-four.

Scattered around the bodies were love letters that apparently had been exchanged by the victims. These letters indicated that the two had been having a passionate affair for several years. They had been remarkably discreet, for no one in the small town of New Brunswick seems to have suspected anything for a long time. But obviously someone found out.

The tiny New Brunswick police force was not experienced in dealing with bizarre murders, indeed in dealing with any kind of murders. They bungled the case right from the start. Local police made only a cursory search of the crime scene, and then they didn't bother to cordon it off. Within a few days the area was overrun with sightseers and souvenir hunters. If there had been any additional evidence it had surely disappeared. New Brunswick it seems simply wanted the whole horrible crime to go away.

In New York, however, Hearst's *Mirror* and other tabloids were engaged in a vicious circulation war. They knew a good circulation-building story when they saw one. Reporters swarmed all over New Brunswick looking for people to interview. The Mills's teenage daughter, who was described as "a jazz-baby flapper who craved notoriety," was a good interview subject. She seemed willing to say almost anything.

The Reverend Hall's widow refused to speak to the press, but her bug-collecting brother, Willie Stevens, who was regarded as a buffoon by the reporters, was always good copy.

In order to bring the matter to some sort of a conclusion a grand jury was convened. The members of the jury came primarily from Mrs. Hall's social circle, and they were presented with very little evidence. Mrs. Hall, an obvious suspect, was not even called to testify. The grand jury quickly pronounced the case unsolved, and the police let the matter drop claiming they had no other avenues of investigation to pursue. Mrs. Hall sailed off to Europe for a long vacation.

But it was just too juicy of a case to be forgotten and four years later, when another circulation war broke out among New York tabloids, the *Mirror* decided to take another look. There wasn't much evidence left, but a private investigator hired by the *Mirror* gained possession of the calling card that had been left at Reverend Hall's shoe. When it was tested for fingerprints it was found to contain those of Mrs. Hall's slow-witted brother Willie Stevens. The press was now in full cry, and fearing bad publicity the state of New Jersey reopened the case. Four people were arrested and charged with a murder plot: Mrs. Hall, Willie Stevens, another brother Henry Stevens, and a cousin, Wall Street financier Henry Carpender.

The newspapers immediately dubbed the proceedings the "Trial of the Century." It was not only the New York tabloids that were interested. Nearly every newspaper in America covered the story. During the trial's twenty-two-day run there were as many as 200 reporters milling around the small town looking for something new to report. Among those who covered the trial were American journalistic icon H. L. Mencken, mystery writer Mary Roberts Rinehart, the sage of Broadway Damon Runyon, as well as antiliquor evangelist Billy Sunday. The murdered Mrs. Mills's husband was recruited as a reporter and his copy was typed by his flapper daughter. It has been estimated that over 12 million words of copy per day were filed during the trial. Sixty leased telegraph wires in the courtroom basement hummed twenty-four hours a day, all funneled through a giant switchboard that had originally been built for coverage of a heavyweight championship fight in Philadelphia.[1] The only really new evidence presented at the trial was the testimony of Mrs. Jane Gibson, who lived near the scene of the crime. She said that on the day of the murder she heard people arguing and the sound of gunshots, and she saw Mrs. Hall's car parked nearby.

Mrs. Gibson raised hogs and the press dubbed her "the pig woman." What made her testimony really dramatic, however, was that she was dying of cancer. She was carried into the courtroom in her hospital bed—and her testimony was described as coming from her deathbed. (Actually she didn't die until four years after the trial.)

The local jury, however, was unmoved and returned not guilty verdicts on all four defendants in a matter of hours.

The *Mirror* had been so convinced of Mrs. Hall's guilt that the editors had been convicting her on their front page for months. The managing editor of the *Mirror* had dared Mrs. Hall to sue the paper. After her acquittal she did, for three million dollars. The *Mirror* was forced to settle out of court, reputedly for a large amount.

Officially the murder has never been solved.

THE LINDBERGH BABY KIDNAPPING

In some respects Charles Lindbergh himself was a creation of the media. His solo nonstop flight across the Atlantic in 1927 was an act of great courage and skill mixed with more than a small amount of luck. But the amount of public attention and adulation Lindbergh received was far out of proportion to the real importance of his achievement. The newspapers and the newer media of radio and newsreel made Lindbergh the greatest American hero of his time. His name is still well known today.

Fame has its hazards as well as its rewards. On the night of March 1, 1932, twenty-month-old Charles Lindbergh Jr. was kidnapped from the Lindbergh country home outside Hopewell, New Jersey. A ransom note had been left on the windowsill and a homemade ladder lay on the ground near the side of the house.

The Lindbergh baby kidnapping was almost immediately labeled the "Crime of the Century" by a hysterical press. Under enormous pressure from the press and public and Lindbergh himself, a frantic investigation began

WANTED

INFORMATION AS TO THE WHEREABOUTS OF

CHAS. A. LINDBERGH, JR.

OF HOPEWELL, N. J.

SON OF COL. CHAS. A. LINDBERGH

World-Famous Aviator

This child was kidnaped from his home in Hopewell, N. J., between 8 and 10 p. m. on Tuesday, March 1, 1932.

DESCRIPTION:

Age, 20 months	Hair, blond, curly
Weight, 27 to 30 lbs.	Eyes, dark blue
Height, 29 inches	Complexion, light

Deep dimple in center of chin
Dressed in one-piece coverall night suit

ADDRESS ALL COMMUNICATIONS TO
COL. H. N. SCHWARZKOPF, TRENTON, N. J., or
COL. CHAS. A. LINDBERGH, HOPEWELL, N. J.

ALL COMMUNICATIONS WILL BE TREATED IN CONFIDENCE

March 11, 1932

COL. H. NORMAN SCHWARZKOPF
Supt. New Jersey State Police, Trenton, N. J.

and quickly became badly confused as local and state authorities clashed with one another over jurisdiction. Newspapers and private individuals tried to carry out their own investigations and posted their own rewards. Even Chicago gangster Al Capone offered to help. As a result much time and important evidence may have been damaged or lost. The coverage of the case was a mixture of genuine journalistic concern and sheer sensationalism. It was often tasteless. Members of the press literally tripped over one another to report every morsel of fact or rumor no matter how intrusive, hurtful, or just plain false.

In April a go-between paid $50,000 to a mysterious man known only as Cemetery John in the Woodlawn Cemetery in the Bronx, New York. The mysterious man seemed to have genuine knowledge of the events of the kidnapping. The child was supposed to be returned, but Cemetery John was never heard from again.

On May 12 the little boy's body was found, covered with leaves, just 4 miles (6 kilometers) from the Lindbergh home. An autopsy showed that his skull had been badly fractured. The entire nation seemed to go into mourning, followed by intense rage.

But it was two and a half years before there was any break in the case. A man named Bruno Richard Hauptmann paid for gas at a Bronx gas station with a bill from the ransom money. A search of the itinerant carpenter's home turned up more of the ransom money plus other evidence apparently linking him to the crime. Hauptmann, who had come to the United States illegally, had a long record of crime in his native Germany.[2]

The new "trial of the century" for the "crime of the century" was held in Flemington, New Jersey, in 1935.

The media gather in Hopewell, New Jersey,
to cover the Lindbergh baby kidnapping.

What can now properly be called not just press but media attention was unprecedented. In addition to newspaper reporters and still photographers, there were radio reporters and newsreel cameramen. Celebrity reporters like Walter Winchell and the presence of newsreel cameras in the courtroom helped to turn the scene into a circus. Some cameramen toured the streets of Flemington with a camera truck, asking passersby to cast their vote about Hauptmann's guilt or innocence for the benefit of the sound newsreel cameras. Newsreel coverage was so intense and so intrusive that the prosecutor tried to pressure the film industry to withdraw the cameras. Some film companies agreed, others did not.[3]

There seemed little doubt that Hauptmann would be convicted and sentenced to death, which is what happened. The case against him was not as strong as prosecutors would have liked, and they are now known to have cut legal corners. Hauptmann continued to maintain his innocence, even after the governor of New Jersey offered to commute his death sentence to life imprisonment if he confessed. So some controversy over the verdict remains, but on balance it seems that he was guilty as charged.

Paramount even managed to get a camera on death row, in defiance of all prison regulations, for a sound interview with Hauptmann in his cell as he awaited execution. Paramount never revealed how it was able to secure this morbidly absorbing footage.

THE SAM SHEPPARD CASE

The case of the murder of Marilyn Sheppard lacked the bizarre quality of the Hall-Mills murder, or the celebrity side of the Lindbergh case—yet in the mid-1950s this case gripped America, and if it did not quite result in another "trial of the century" it was surely the trial of the decade. And it was a telling example of sensationalized media coverage, even in an era that was considered calm, highly moral, and nonsensational.

On July 4, 1954, Marilyn Sheppard was battered to death in her home in the quiet, affluent Cleveland suburb of Bay Village. Her husband, Dr. Sam Sheppard, a popular and prominent osteopathic surgeon, said that he had heard his wife scream and rushed up to the bedroom. He was then struck from behind and knocked unconscious. When he regained consciousness he said that he chased a "bushy haired" man out of the house to the lakefront, where he was hit and again knocked unconscious.

At first "Dr. Sam," as he was almost universally called, was regarded as a second victim. But the police soon became suspicious of his story. The murder weapon could not be found and there were no fingerprints of outsiders found in the house. The police quickly came to believe that Dr. Sam had used the time between the attack and when the police were finally notified to dispose of the murder weapon and cover up any other incriminating evidence, as well as to feign his own injuries.

On July 16, an editorial in the *Cleveland Press* attacked "the tragic mishandling of the Sheppard murder investigation." Four days later a banner headline declared that Sheppard was "Getting Away With Murder."

What really sealed Sheppard's fate, however, was the revelation that he had been having a longtime affair with Susan Hayes, a former laboratory technician at Bay View hospital, which was owned by Sheppard and his doctor brothers. Public opinion turned sharply against "Dr. Sam."

This rather ordinary and unremarkable crime caught the public fancy and the Sheppard trial attracted a huge crowd of reporters from around the country, including journalistic stars like Dorothy Kilgallen, Hearst's top "sob sister" and a popular television personality in her own right. In a media circus atmosphere Sam Sheppard was convicted and sentenced to life in prison.

The case should have ended there, but it didn't. The case was taken up by the popular mystery writer Erle Stanley Gardner, creator of Perry Mason, in his *Argosy* magazine column, "The Court of Last Resort." Gardner found experts who would testify that local police had completely bungled the investigation and that prosecutors had suppressed evidence that might have exonerated Dr. Sam. Once again the case was all over the media.

In June 1966, Sheppard was granted a new trial by the U.S. Supreme Court, which ruled that his right to a fair trial had been violated by prejudicial news coverage. At his second trial Sheppard was represented by an aggressive, ambitious, and media-savvy young defense lawyer named F. Lee Bailey, who was out to make his own reputation. Bailey hinted that a woman had committed the crime.[4]

This time Dr. Sam was found not guilty. He had his medical license restored and moved back to Bay Village with his new European wife, who had read about the case in a German magazine. But Sheppard's life quickly fell apart. His wife divorced him and he was dogged by medical malpractice suits. He gave up medicine, took up team wrestling and motorcycle riding, and married the young daughter of friends who had taken him into their home. He died in 1970 at the age of forty-six.

The defendant was dead but the case didn't die. It was the basis for an extremely popular television series of the 1960s, "The Fugitive," remade into a popular movie in the 1990s.

Dr. Sheppard's son has devoted much of his life to proving his father's innocence. He has written a book claiming that the real killer was an Ohio convict named Richard Eberling who had worked briefly at the Sheppard house. Before he died, Eberling allegedly confessed to a fellow inmate that he had committed the crime. Ohio legal authorities are unimpressed and though the case is still officially open they think they had the right man in the first place and there is no active investigation. We are not likely to ever know any more about the crime than we do today.

THE O. J. TRIAL

As the century drew to a close there was a new "trial of the century." This time the title was not an exaggeration. For the modern yellow journalist it was a case that had everything: murder, sex, celebrity, race, and hints of vast conspiracies.

On the night of June 12, 1994, Los Angeles police were called to investigate a bloody scene in the posh suburb of Brentwood. In the courtyard of an upscale condominium they found the bodies of two people, a man and a woman, who had been slashed to death. The woman was quickly identified as Nicole Brown Simpson, who lived in the building. The man was Ron Goldman, waiter in an area restaurant.

From the start it was clear to everyone that this was going to be a sensational case because the woman was the estranged wife of O. J. Simpson, a former football star turned actor and celebrity pitchman. O. J. was one of the best-known and most popular figures in America. He was also African American and his wife, Nicole, was white.

O. J. immediately became the prime suspect. What the police knew, and the public did not, was that O. J. and his wife had long been locked in a violent relationship. Simpson had actually pled guilty to beating his wife, though this had attracted scant press attention when it happened. O. J.'s alibi for the time of the murder was shaky and evidence had been found both at the crime scene and at O. J.'s home just a short distance away that linked him to the crime.

On June 17, Simpson's lawyer was told that his client had been charged with first-degree murder and should surrender to the police. His lawyer said that Simpson would turn himself in, but he didn't. Instead he left what sounded like a suicide note and made a run for it. His car, a very conspicuous white Ford Bronco, was spotted by

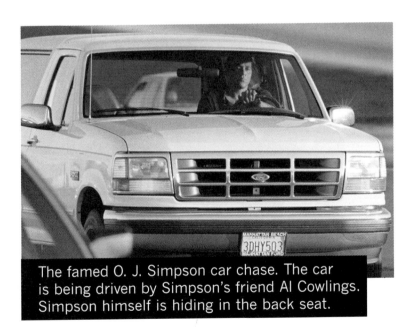

The famed O. J. Simpson car chase. The car is being driven by Simpson's friend Al Cowlings. Simpson himself is hiding in the back seat.

police and followed at a slow speed by a convoy of police cars. This bizarre event was picked up by TV crews in helicopters and broadcast live on all three networks and several cable channels in prime time. NBC even cut away from broadcast of an NBA championship game. Ninety-five million people watched the slow 60-mile (90-kilometer) procession down a Los Angeles freeway and back to Brentwood. Television made all the difference. Some people near the freeway who had been alerted to the event by television rushed out to cheer or hold up signs supporting Simpson. Live coverage was helping to make the news.[5]

Reading a written report of the event in a newspaper, even with photographs, listening to a live radio report, or seeing videotaped snippets on the evening news lacked the impact of live television. The enormous attention attracted by this event was an unmistakable sign that what was unfolding was going to be a lot more than just another celebrity murder case.

As the case came to trial, presiding judge Lance Ito made a fateful decision: He agreed that all the courtroom proceedings could be televised. Whether to allow cameras in the courtroom has been a controversial subject for years. Some courts will not even allow still photographers, and for illustrations newspapers must rely on courtroom sketch artists just as they had a century earlier. But gradually cameras in the courtroom had been gaining acceptance by everyone.

Allowing the trial to be televised was an idea that initially was favored by both defense and prosecution. The hope was that if people could see what actually went on there would be less sensationalized interpretation and the process would seem more honest and open. That's not the way it worked out.

The trial of O. J. Simpson began in January 1995 and stretched on for nine months, far longer than anyone had expected. Every moment of it was shown on live television. In fact, many pretrial courtroom actions were also televised live. The networks didn't broadcast everything, but several cable channels like CNN and Court TV covered the trial from gavel to gavel.

In addition there were countless courthouse steps interviews with lawyers for both sides putting their own spin on events. After the big show was over there were the panel shows where the events of the day were rehashed by a revolving panel of "experts"– lawyers, ex-judges, journalists, witnesses, and others, many of whom became celebrities themselves. For almost a year American television was dominated by the Simpson trial twenty-four hours a day. The area in front of the courtroom filled with television satellite trucks and hordes of reporters and cameramen waiting for something, anything to happen was christened "Camp O. J." or "O. J. City." At slack times reporters were reduced to interviewing one another.

The newspapers and newsmagazines could not really compete with the wall-to-wall live coverage of the trial that television provided, but many of them tried. The supermarket tabloids and some of the tabloid TV shows, however, did actually have an impact on how the trial was conducted. Mainstream news publications and television news should not pay for an interview or other information. The tabloids, however, do and in a sensational case like this one they were willing to pay a great deal of money for an exclusive.

Before and during the trial a number of potential witnesses sold their personal stories to the tabloids. As soon as it was known that an individual had been paid, their potential credibility as a witness was damaged and they were not even called to testify. As a result some important testimony may have been kept out of the trial.

After a trial lasting nine months and mountains of testimony it took the jury less than four hours to reach a verdict. The judge unaccountably delayed announcing the verdict until the following day. Anticipation built up overnight, and the live televised reading of the verdict drew more viewers in America than any other event in history. Simpson was found not guilty on both counts of murder.

Reaction to the verdict was split. Most African Americans applauded it, while most whites were appalled, not only at the verdict but at the speed with which it had been reached. There was a lot of bitterness, but no outbreaks of violence that had accompanied other racially charged, high-profile cases.

The story wasn't over; there was a civil trial. In 1996 the families of the victims brought wrongful death suits against Simpson. This time the trial was very different. The unprecedented attention the first trial had received was widely criticized. It had caused many who had originally favored cameras in the courtroom to change their opinion. The judge in this case barred cameras and imposed tough gag orders on the lawyers. There was still plenty of coverage of this trial, but the near frenzy of 1995 was not repeated.

The trial verdict was very different as well. This time O. J. Simpson was found "liable" on both counts of "wrongful death"–which was simply another way of say-

The Simpson trial made the covers of the major news magazines for months and months.

ing that this jury found him guilty of murder. A hastily arranged two-hour "Rivera Live" show on the civil trial verdict was seen in two million American homes. It was the largest audience for any cable TV show except professional wrestling.

The entirely opposite verdicts have been explained in a variety of ways. New evidence was presented in the second trial. Simpson himself was forced to testify, and did poorly. The judge in the second trial controlled the trial much more closely and did not allow much peripheral information to come into the trial. The venue of the trial may also have been critical. The first trial was held in Los Angeles itself and the jury was overwhelmingly African American. The civil trial was held in the affluent area where the crime had actually been committed and the jury was overwhelmingly white. The importance of the

Former intern Monica Lewinsky and her father make their way through a crowd of reporters.

racial makeup of the different juries in determining the opposite verdicts in the two cases is a matter that was much discussed and debated.

But after the second verdict something happened that at one time had not seemed possible. The case that had dominated the media and obsessed the public for almost two years simply fell out of the news. There was the occasional story, but even that became less and less common.

There had been a virtual flood of books by practically everyone connected with the case: reporters, novelists, jurors, witnesses, lawyers, policemen, and former prosecutors. Books that came out late in the cycle simply did not sell.

A long and sometimes revealing interview with Simpson himself made by a British television company wasn't even fully broadcast in the United States. At one time such an interview would have been headline news. Now very few were interested.

Experienced yellow journalists could have predicted what happened. They knew that no matter how sensational a story is for a while, eventually the public gets bored. They have heard it all before and are on the lookout for a new sensation. There were new murders to be discussed, new trials to be covered. That's what happened with the O. J. Simpson case. It had a good run, but it became "old news" and the public simply forgot about it.

The O. J. case did not change the country. It did, however, influence the nature of sensational journalism, particularly on television. The programs that had once been practically all O. J. all the time turned to new sensational crimes, and ultimately to the scandals swirling around President Bill Clinton. The now familiar experts who had once talked about murder in Brentwood now bickered publicly and endlessly over impeachment in Washington. As in the past, sensation sells, but it has to be a new sensation. Old news gets boring.

The era of the penny press, yellow journalism, and jazz journalism is still with us in a new format, but quite recognizable.

It just hasn't been given a new name yet.

NOTES

Chapter 1
1. Daniel Cohen, *Monsters, Giants and Little Men From Mars* (New York: Doubleday, 1975), pp. 191-92.
2. Edwin Emery, *The Press in America* (Englewood Cliffs, NJ: Prentice-Hall, 1972), p. 167.
3. Emery, p. 170.
4. W. A. Swanberg, *Citizen Hearst* (New York: Scribners, 1961), pp. 287–88.
5. Daniel Cohen, *Henry Stanley* (New York: Evans, 1985), p. 55.

Chapter 2
1. W. A. Swanberg, *Citizen Hearst* (New York: Scribners, 1961), p. 192.
2. Swanberg, p. 43.
3. Ben Procter, *William Randolph Hearst, The Early Years* (New York: Oxford Press, 1998), p. 78.
4. Swanberg, p. 50.
5. Swanberg, p. 69.
6. Edwin Emery, *The Press in America* (Englewood Cliffs, NJ: Prentice-Hall, 1972), p. 365.
7. Swanberg, p. 172.
8. Swanberg, p. 82.

Chapter 3
1. Fred W. Friendly, *Minnesota Rag* (New York: Vintage, 1982), p. 29.
2. Friendly, p. 16.
3. Richard Norton Smith, *The Colonel: The life and Legend of Robert R. McCormick* (Boston: Houghton Mifflin, 1997), p. 281.
4. Friendly, p. 150.
5. Friendly, p. 151.

Chapter 4

1. Neal Gabler, *Winchell: Gossip, Power and the Culture of Celebrity* (New York: Knopf, 1994), p. XI.
2. Gabler, p. 63.
3. Gabler, p. 66.
4. Bernard Weintraub, "He Turned Gossip into Tawdry Power," *The New York Times* (Nov. 18, 1998), p. E1.
5. Gabler, p. 162.
6. Weintraub, p. E3.
7. Weintraub, p. E3.

Chapter 5

1. Edwin Emery, *The Press in America* (Englewood Cliffs, NJ: Prentice-Hall, 1972), p. 560.
2. Emery, p. 555.
3. Weegee, *Naked City*, (New York: Dutton, 1945), p. 43.
4. Weegee, p. 9.
5. Peter Plagens, "Cutting to the Chase," *Newsweek* (Sept. 22, 1997), p. 86.
6. Fred Tasker, "World Media Face a Soul-Searching Question," Knight Ridder/Tribune News Service (Sept. 3, 1997).

Chapter 6

1. Raymond Fielding, *The American Newsreel* (Norman: University of Oklahoma Press, 1972), p. 114.
2. Elizabeth Gleick, "Geraldo Rivera: Fresh From a Triumph in the O. J. Wars," *People* (March 17, 1997), p. 99.
3. Howard Chua-Eoan, "Too Many Eyes in the Sky," *Time* (May 11, 1998), p. 30.
4. Tech Web, "The World-Wide Winchells," www.cmpnet.com, The Technology Network (Aug. 18, 1998).
5. Tech Web.

Chapter 7

1. Edwin Emery, *The Press in America* (Englewood Cliffs, NJ: Prentice-Hall, 1972), p. 559.
2. Jay Robert Nash, *Almanac of World Crime* (New York: Doubleday/Anchor, 1981), p. 216.
3. Raymond Fielding, *The American Newsreel* (Norman: University of Oklahoma Press, 1972), p. 210.
4. *Crimes of the 20th Century* (New York: Random House, 1991), p. 179.
5. Earle Rice Jr., *The O. J. Simpson Trial* (San Diego, CA: Lucent Books, 1997), p. 35.

BIBLIOGRAPHY

Clark, Marcia. *Without a Doubt.* New York: Viking, 1997.

Cohen, Daniel. *Henry Stanley.* New York: Evans, 1985.

———. *Monsters, Giants and Little Men from Mars.* New York: Doubleday, 1975.

Crimes of the 20th Century. New York: Random House, 1991.

Emery, Edwin. *The Press and America* (3rd edition). Englewood Cliffs, NJ: Prentice Hall, 1972.

Fielding, Raymond. *The American Newsreel.* Norman: University of Oklahoma Press, 1972.

Friendly, Fred W. *Minnesota Rag.* New York: Vintage, 1982.

Gabler, Neal. *Winchell: Gossip, Power and the Culture of Celebrity.* New York: Knopf, 1994.

Klurfeld, Herman. *Winchell: His Life and Times.* New York: Prager, 1976.

Nash, Jay Robert. *Almanac of World Crime.* New York: Doubleday/Anchor, 1981.

Procter, Ben. *William Randolph Hearst, The Early Years.* New York: Oxford Press, 1998.

Rice, Earle Jr. *The O.J. Simpson Trial.* San Diego, CA: Lucent Books, 1997.

Smith, Richard Norton. *The Colonel: The Life and Legend of Robert R. McCormick.* Boston: Houghton Mifflin, 1997.

Swanberg, W. A. *Citizen Hearst.* New York: Scribners, 1961.

Weegee. *Naked City.* New York: Dutton, 1945.

Winchell, Walter. *Winchell Exclusive.* Englewood Cliffs, NJ: Prentice-Hall, 1975.

INDEX